Ethics in Business

ISSUES

Volume 227

Series Editor
Lisa Firth

Educational Publishers
Cambridge

First published by Independence

The Studio, High Green

Great Shelford

Cambridge CB22 5EG

England

British Library Cataloguing in Publication Data

Ethics in business. – (Issues ; v. 227)

1. Social responsibility of business--Great Britain.

I. Series II. Firth, Lisa.

658.4'08'0941-dc23

ISBN-13: 978 1 86168 616 9

Printed in Great Britain

MWL Print Group Ltd

CONTENTS

Chapter 1 Business in the UK

Chapter 2 Corporate Responsibility

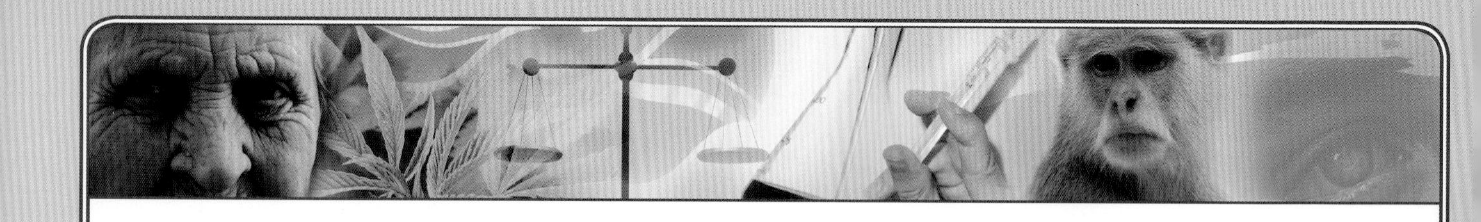

OTHER TITLES IN THE ISSUES SERIES

For more on these titles, visit: www.independence.co.uk

The Internet Revolution ISBN 978 1 86168 451 6
An Ageing Population ISBN 978 1 86168 452 3
Poverty and Exclusion ISBN 978 1 86168 453 0
Waste Issues ISBN 978 1 86168 454 7
Staying Fit ISBN 978 1 86168 455 4
The AIDS Crisis ISBN 978 1 86168 468 4
Bullying Issues ISBN 978 1 86168 469 1
Marriage and Cohabitation ISBN 978 1 86168 470 7
Privacy and Surveillance ISBN 978 1 86168 472 1
The Animal Rights Debate ISBN 978 1 86168 473 8
Body Image and Self-Esteem ISBN 978 1 86168 484 4
Abortion – Rights and Ethics ISBN 978 1 86168 485 1
Racial and Ethnic Discrimination ISBN 978 1 86168 486 8
Sexual Health ISBN 978 1 86168 487 5
Selling Sex ISBN 978 1 86168 488 2
Citizenship and Participation ISBN 978 1 86168 489 9
Health Issues for Young People ISBN 978 1 86168 500 1
Reproductive Ethics ISBN 978 1 86168 502 5
Tackling Child Abuse ISBN 978 1 86168 503 2
Money and Finances ISBN 978 1 86168 504 9
The Housing Issue ISBN 978 1 86168 505 6
Teenage Conceptions ISBN 978 1 86168 523 0
Work and Employment ISBN 978 1 86168 524 7
Understanding Eating Disorders ISBN 978 1 86168 525 4
Student Matters ISBN 978 1 86168 526 1
Cannabis Use ISBN 978 1 86168 527 8
Health and the State ISBN 978 1 86168 528 5
Tobacco and Health ISBN 978 1 86168 539 1
The Homeless Population ISBN 978 1 86168 540 7
Coping with Depression ISBN 978 1 86168 541 4
The Changing Family ISBN 978 1 86168 542 1
Bereavement and Grief ISBN 978 1 86168 543 8
Endangered Species ISBN 978 1 86168 544 5
Responsible Drinking ISBN 978 1 86168 555 1
Alternative Medicine ISBN 978 1 86168 560 5
Censorship Issues ISBN 978 1 86168 558 2
Living with Disability ISBN 978 1 86168 557 5
Sport and Society ISBN 978 1 86168 559 9
Self-Harming and Suicide ISBN 978 1 86168 556 8
Sustainable Transport ISBN 978 1 86168 572 8
Mental Wellbeing ISBN 978 1 86168 573 5
Child Exploitation ISBN 978 1 86168 574 2
The Gambling Problem ISBN 978 1 86168 575 9
The Energy Crisis ISBN 978 1 86168 576 6
Nutrition and Diet ISBN 978 1 86168 577 3
Coping with Stress ISBN 978 1 86168 582 7
Consumerism and Ethics ISBN 978 1 86168 583 4
Genetic Modification ISBN 978 1 86168 584 1
Education and Society ISBN 978 1 86168 585 8
The Media ISBN 978 1 86168 586 5
Biotechnology and Cloning ISBN 978 1 86168 587 2
International Terrorism ISBN 978 1 86168 592 6
The Armed Forces ISBN 978 1 86168 593 3
Vegetarian Diets ISBN 978 1 86168 594 0
Religion in Society ISBN 978 1 86168 595 7
Tackling Climate Change ISBN 978 1 86168 596 4
Euthanasia and Assisted Suicide ISBN 978 1 86168 597 1
A Sustainable Future ISBN 978 1 86168 603 9
Class and Social Mobility ISBN 978 1 86168 604 6
Population Growth and Migration ISBN 978 1 86168 605 3
Equality and Gender Roles ISBN 978 1 86168 606 0
Tourism and Travel ISBN 978 1 86168 607 7
Crime, Punishment and Justice ISBN 978 1 86168 608 4
Domestic and Relationship Abuse ISBN 978 1 86168 613 8
LGBT Equality ISBN 978 1 86168 614 5
Globalisation and Trade ISBN 978 1 86168 615 2
Ethics in Business ISBN 978 1 86168 616 9
Illegal Drug Use ISBN 978 1 86168 617 6
Protecting Human Rights ISBN 978 1 86168 618 3

A note on critical evaluation

Because the information reprinted here is from a number of different sources, readers should bear in mind the origin of the text and whether the source is likely to have a particular bias when presenting information (just as they would if undertaking their own research). It is hoped that, as you read about the many aspects of the issues explored in this book, you will critically evaluate the information presented. It is important that you decide whether you are being presented with facts or opinions. Does the writer give a biased or an unbiased report? If an opinion is being expressed, do you agree with the writer?

Ethics in Business offers a useful starting point for those who need convenient access to information about the many issues involved. However, it is only a starting point. Following each article is a URL to the relevant organisation's website, which you may wish to visit for further information.

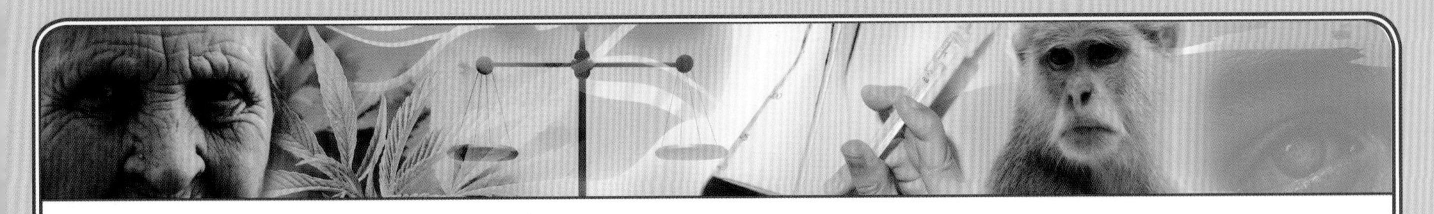

BUSINESS IN THE UK

Brave new world of business

How is technology, globalisation and the environment affecting the way we work? Vanessa Townsend reports.

Predicting the future is not an exact science. However, in these days of rapidly changing technology, it has become more imperative than ever for companies to look ahead and try and predict how technological advances, globalisation, environmental concerns and people's desire for more flexible working will affect the way business is carried out. And this future of work matters not only in the way we work but where we work.

In fact, commentators predict that for firms, the next decade will be as revolutionary as the original Industrial Revolution nearly three centuries ago and this time it's global. In *McKinsey Quarterly*, an online business journal, W Brian Arthur, in his essay 'The second economy', argues that the Internet and digitisation is the biggest change since the Industrial Revolution: 'In fact, I think it may well be the biggest change ever in the economy... There's no upper limit to this, no place where it has to end.' Professor Lynda Gratton in her book *The Shift* believes that due to technology, 'the world is at the apex of an enormously creative and innovative shift that will result in profound changes to the everyday lives of people across the world'.

Matt Barrie, chief executive of online outsourcing marketplace Freelancer.com, agrees that technology is changing rapidly – and transforming the way we do business. 'The Internet is the next shift,' he told Recruiter. 'There's still 70% of the world's seven billion population about to join the Internet.' He gave the example of the Philippines, where in 2009, eight million Filipinos were on the Internet. 'In 2010 that figure is around 30 million,' he says. 'Technology will massively change the way we do our jobs, and that's an inevitable fact.'

The trend is expanding exponentially. Kjetil Olsen, vice-president (Europe) at online employment site Elance, says: 'More and more individuals are choosing the freelance lifestyle that gives them freedom to work when they want, where they want and with whom they want. The freelancing model also provides the opportunity to specialise and work on projects they love. Using the UK as an example, the Professional Contractors Group (PCG) estimates there are 1.4 million freelancers now working in the UK, with that number set to grow substantially over the next decade.'

According to a new book by senior visiting fellow at Cass Business School, Alison Maitland, and Peter Thomson, visiting executive fellow at Henley Business School (*Future Work: How Businesses Can Adapt and Thrive In The New World Of Work*), employees are more productive if they have greater autonomy over where, when and how they work. The growth of 'future work' will also see more work being done remotely and more 'work hubs' – specially designed workspaces equipped with the technology to support mobile workers, says Maitland. 'Instead of being the location where employees gather at fixed times to do concentrated work, the office could become primarily a place for developing and maintaining connections between people,' she adds.

RECRUITER

This rise in a more 'entrepreneurial' way of working is happening globally, particularly with the cost of computers and more importantly mobile devices becoming ever more affordable, including for those in growing economies. Gratton told Recruiter at the launch of Phase 3 of the Future of Work Consortium in London last month that today in the UK, the US and Europe, it is the SMEs and not the big corporations that are creating the jobs. A recent report by Bibby Financial Services, *2020 Vision: The Future of Business*, also predicts a 20% increase in the number of small businesses in the UK. Yet by the end of the decade, even though these businesses will be the main hirers, the way employees work and where they work could look very different compared to today's workplace.

Much of this shift is as a result of the ability to work 'in the cloud'. Employees can today work from anywhere without restriction and this is forecast to increase exponentially. Managing director of cloud computing specialists virtualDCS, Richard May, believes there will be an increase in remote teams working in a collaborative fashion: 'I think large businesses will still be around, but the necessity for them to all be working from the same place will greatly reduce. Online collaborative working is now mainstream, with services like Skype, Meetme and PowWowNow providing easy consumer access to services such as video conferencing and shared desktops.'

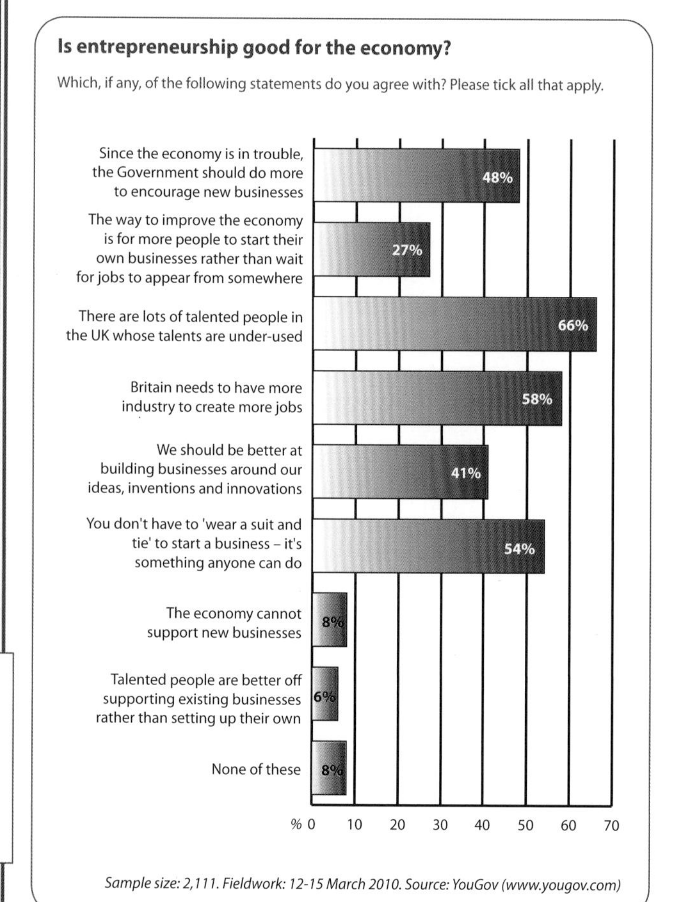

Sample size: 2,111. Fieldwork: 12-15 March 2010. Source: YouGov (www.yougov.com)

Futurist at TomorrowToday, Dean van Leeuwen, predicts that the daily routine tasks of people will be managed and monitored more and more by artificial intelligent computer programs. 'Advanced learning algorithms could, within the next decade or two, actually monitor and manage progress against set tasks and agreed output,' he told Recruiter. 'Leaders would be freed up to motivate, engage with and strategise, rather than clock watch people, freeing up time for what humans are best at – finding creative solutions.'

This rise in a more 'entrepreneurial' way of working is happening globally

This would undoubtedly mean a whole new approach in employee structure of a business, he explains: 'Companies could be managed with a core set of senior managers, mainly financial analysts and strategists, with tasks from marketing to HR being outsourced to freelancers who would bid for work. These flexible teams would come together to form temporary units that complete a task or project and then abandon, perhaps to reform on another project "set". The best talent would be bid for and those that constantly deliver will command the highest wages.'

Maitland adds that employers will increasingly be looking to recruit people with the management skills needed for future work: 'As for new recruits to the workforce, employers will be looking for self-starters who are happy to be measured and rewarded by results, not hours put in, and who are adaptable to working in much more flexible ways. This is what many of the digital generation want anyway, and the greatest adjustment is likely to have to come from established, older managers than from the younger generation.'

For smaller businesses, the cost of hiring premises, particularly in major cities, is prohibitive and will be increasingly so. Graham Ventham is director of Conrad Consulting, specialist recruiters for civil and structural engineers. The firm has a virtual office address in the City of London. 'We're based out in Suffolk and we just find it more professional to have a London address,' he told Recruiter. 'Even with services in the cloud, there is still a need for a London address. We use the meeting rooms on an *ad hoc* basis either for interviewing candidates or for our clients to carry out interviews. We're really pleased with the service it provides.'

Conrad Consulting has been a virtual customer of serviced and virtual offices provider Executive Offices Group for about two years. Chief executive John Drover has seen a 30% increase in virtual office use in the last 12 months. In the next five years or so, he believes many

RECRUITER

smaller organisations will specialise in certain sectors and partner with other small firms to add value to their proposition. 'This will challenge the medium-sized firms with their rigid structure and fixed overheads,' he told Recruiter. 'People will work remotely for some of the time but ultimately humans like to cross the motivational divide and work collaboratively on a face-to-face basis.'

However, David Howell, owner and MD of financial executive search firm EM Group, says that for his sector there needs to be a physical central London presence. But he adds that with cloud computing, headhunters can work independently. 'There are lots of caveats around that,' he told Recruiter. 'You need maturity, trust and regular appraisals to allow consultants to work flexibly. We've found a way that works.' He explains that this model of working evolved, which was made easier by the technology and the high levels of support from their cloud specialist partner, virtualDCS. 'Now the concept has been established, we are clear it only works when there is a mature, trust-based culture, backed up with regular face-to-face accountability sessions,' he says. 'So going forward, we will only hire those with whom we can be comfortable on this point.'

Earlier this year a joint report from virtual office provider Regus and work and technology specialist Unwired, *VWork: Winning Strategies at Work*, raised the future spectre of the death of the office and emphasised the growing role of the 'third space' not working from home or even a virtual office but at the local coffee shop, shopping centre or the library, anywhere where there was access to the virtual world.

And Gratton was recently interviewed by an Indian magazine, which features people in their offices. 'We had to do four different pictures,' she says. 'I work at home, I have an office at London Business School, the Future of Work offices are in Somerset House [on the Strand in London] and I write books at my place in Spain. The idea of one office with a desk is becoming quite antiquated.'

This fundamental change in the way we will be working, as well as raising the possibility of using different criteria for interviewing the new employee of the future, may also give rise to how business and recruiters go about hiring. Olsen believes that more and more businesses in the future will use online employment platforms to hire employees, making working online not only easier, but also necessary to do business effectively.

He says that sites such as Elance and Freelancer.com will be an integral part of hiring practices at SMEs as more businesses adopt an online work model. 'It should not just be considered outsourcing, it is actually online employment,' he explains, 'a smart, cost-effective way to hire and manage distributed teams to get work done in a cost-effective way. Just as e-commerce brought shopping for goods and services into the living room, [online] platforms can give any company, small or large, access to the top talent they need.'

2 November 2011

⇨ The above information is reprinted with kind permission from Recruiter. For more information on the recruitment industry, see www.recruiter.co.uk

UK economy key facts

Information from the Foreign and Commonwealth Office.

- ⇨ The UK is the world's sixth largest economy and one of the world's top ten manufacturers.
- ⇨ The UK is the world's second largest services exporter and the world's sixth largest trading nation.
- ⇨ The World Bank rated the UK second in the EU and seventh in the world on its 'Ease of Doing Business' ranking.
- ⇨ The UK is the number one location for European headquarters: more overseas companies have their European headquarters in the UK than in France and Germany put together.
- ⇨ Six of the world's top ten vehicle makers are based in the UK – the industry accounts for 11% of the UK's manufactured exports.
- ⇨ The UK has the world's second largest aerospace market share, with an annual turnover of £20 billion per year.
- ⇨ London's global financial centre was ranked first in the 2011 Global Financial Centres Index. Across the UK, there are more than one million people employed in financial services.
- ⇨ UK academic institutions include four of the world's top ten universities.
- ⇨ The UK has created five of the world's top 20 best-selling medicines.
- ⇨ The UK's low carbon industry is worth £112 billion per year and employs 910,000 people.

⇨ The above information is reprinted with kind permission from the Foreign and Commonwealth Office. Visit www.fco.gov.uk for more information.

Businesses in the UK

Extract from **Business population estimates for the UK and regions 2011: statistical release.**

- There were an estimated 4.5 million private sector businesses in the UK at the start of 2011, an increase of 94,000 (2.1 per cent) since the start of 2010.
- These businesses employed an estimated 23.4 million people, and had an estimated combined annual turnover of £3,100 billion.[1]
- Almost two-thirds (62.4 per cent) of private sector businesses were sole proprietorships, 27.7 per cent were companies and 9.8 per cent were partnerships.
- Small and medium-sized enterprises (SME)[2] accounted for 99.9 per cent of all enterprises, 58.8 per cent of private sector employment and 48.8 per cent of private sector turnover.

Stock of businesses and their associated employment and turnover

There were an estimated 4.5 million private sector businesses in the UK at the start of 2011, an increase of 94,000 (2.1 per cent) since the start of 2010.[3]

At the start of 2011, the 4.5 million UK private sector enterprises employed an estimated 23.4 million people, and had an estimated combined annual turnover of £3,100 billion.

Almost all of these enterprises (99.2 per cent) were small (0 to 49 employees). Only 30,000 (0.7 per cent) were medium-sized (50 to 249 employees) and 6,000 (0.1 per cent) were large (250 or more employees).

At the start of 2011, the 4.5 million UK private sector SMEs employed an estimated 13.8 million people, and had an estimated combined annual turnover of £1,500 billion.

SMEs together accounted for more than half of employment (58.8 per cent) and almost half of turnover (48.8 per cent) in the UK private sector, at the start of 2011.

Small enterprises alone (0 to 49 employees) accounted for 46.2 per cent of private sector employment and 34.9 per cent of private sector turnover.

Change in the stock of businesses over time

The estimated number of private sector businesses in the UK has increased in each of the last 11 years. At the start of 2011, there were an estimated 4.5 million private sector businesses, an increase of 1.07 million (31.0 per cent) since 2000. Over the last decade, the year-on-year increase in the number of private sector businesses varied between a minimum of 0.1 per cent between the start of 2004 and the start of 2005 and a maximum of 6.9 per cent between the start of 2003 and the start of 2004.

These changes were entirely driven by SMEs – their estimated number increased from 3.5 million to 4.5 million (31.1 per cent) between the start of 2000 and the start of 2011.

Meanwhile, the estimated number of large private sector businesses decreased from 7,200 to 6,300 (-12.0 per cent) over the same period.

The number of businesses with and without employees

At the start of 2011, businesses with employees accounted for over a quarter of all private sector businesses in the UK (25.9 per cent, or 1.2 million enterprises). This represents a fall of 29,000 (-2.4 per cent) since the start of 2010. They employed 19.7 million people and had an estimated combined turnover of £2,900 billion.

At the start of 2011, businesses with no employees[4] accounted for 74.1 per cent of all private sector businesses in the UK (3.4 million enterprises), an increase of 123,000 (3.8 per cent) since the start of 2010. Enterprises with no employees had an estimated combined turnover of £202 billion at the start of 2011.

Legal status of businesses

At the start of 2011, 62.4 per cent of private sector enterprises were sole proprietorships, 27.7 per cent were companies and 9.8 per cent were partnerships.

There were an estimated 2.8 million sole proprietorships in the UK at the start of 2011, of which 279,000 (9.8 per cent) had employees.

There were an estimated 447,000 partnerships, of which 157,000 (35.2 per cent) had employees.

There were 1.3 million companies, of which 742,000 (59.0 per cent) had employees.[5]

Registered and unregistered businesses

The majority of private sector enterprises were unregistered. There were 2,060,000 enterprises (45.3 per cent of all private sector enterprises) registered for VAT and/or PAYE at the start of 2011.

During 2010, the number of sole proprietorships increased by 87,000 (3.2 per cent), the number of partnerships increased by 1,000 (0.2 per cent) and the number of companies increased by 6,000 (0.5 per cent).

DEPARTMENT FOR BUSINESS, INNOVATION AND SKILLS

The number of registered enterprises fell by 33,000 (-1.6 per cent) during 2010, to 2,060,000 at the start of 2011. However, the number of unregistered businesses increased by an estimated 127,000 (5.4 per cent), to reach 2,482,000 at the start of 2011. Most of the change in the number of businesses between 2010 and 2011 was due to an increase in the estimated number of unregistered sole proprietorships (increasing by 113,000, or 5.1 per cent).

Notes

1. Turnover throughout this release excludes SIC2007 Section K (financial and insurance activities) and Division 78 (Employment activities) where data is not available on a comparable basis.
2. In this release, SMEs are defined as having between 0-249 employees. accounted for 99.9 per cent of all enterprises, 58.8 per cent of private sector employment and 48.8 per cent of private sector turnover.
3. This comparison is made using an estimate of the start-2010 stock calculated on a consistent basis, using the BPE 2011 methodology.
4. Enterprises with no employees are either i) sole proprietorships and partnerships comprising only the self-employed owner-manager(s), or ii) companies comprising only one employee director.
5. For legal reasons most companies are run by employees. However, in this publication companies with a single employee director are treated as having no employees.

12 October 2011

➪ The above information is an extract from the Department for Business, Innovation and Skills' statistical release *Business population estimates for the UK and regions*, and is reprinted with permission. Visit www.bis.gov.uk for more information.

Employment in private sector, by number of employees in enterprise

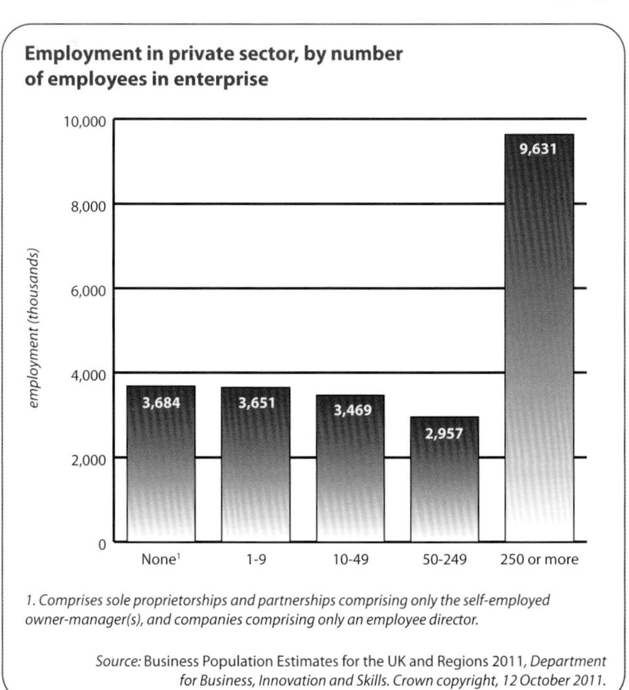

1. Comprises sole proprietorships and partnerships comprising only the self-employed owner-manager(s), and companies comprising only an employee director.

Source: Business Population Estimates for the UK and Regions 2011, *Department for Business, Innovation and Skills. Crown copyright, 12 October 2011.*

Start-ups on the rise in UK

Start-ups in 2011 number an estimated 471,000.

The number of businesses started in 2011 is up by 18 per cent on last year, research finds.

Start-ups in 2011 number an estimated 471,000 compared to around 400,000 in 2010, according to a study by business intelligence firm Creditsafe. By the end of the year, some 16,000 of these are expected to be insolvent.

London is the centre of business start-ups, with almost 160,000 new businesses expected to be set up by the end of the year. The South East is the second most popular location for fledgling businesses (60,715), while the North West will be the hub for more than 46,000 new businesses, followed by East Anglia with more than 40,000.

On a city level, a similar story is revealed, with Greater London top and Birmingham (West Midlands), Manchester (North West) and Guildford (South East) making up the top four. The North East and Northern Ireland are the only regions not to have a representative city in the top 15.

Business development director at Creditsafe David Knowles says, 'This year has been difficult but the entrepreneurial spirit of the Great British public is alive and kicking. While there has been a higher number of business insolvencies this year, the number of new businesses set up over the last two years has also grown steadily. Overall, growth in the UK business population has actually accelerated in 2011.'

Knowles expects that, by the end of the year, more than 14,000 new businesses will have started in Birmingham, 4,000 more than nearest rival Manchester, confirming Birmingham's status as 'second city' of the UK.

'It is perhaps no coincidence that Yorkshire & Humber and the North West – which have seen the biggest public sector job cuts – have also seen significant rises in start-ups. This could suggest that those made redundant in the public sector are starting new ventures in the private sector,' he adds.

5 December 2011

➪ The above information is reprinted with kind permission from SmallBusiness.co.uk.

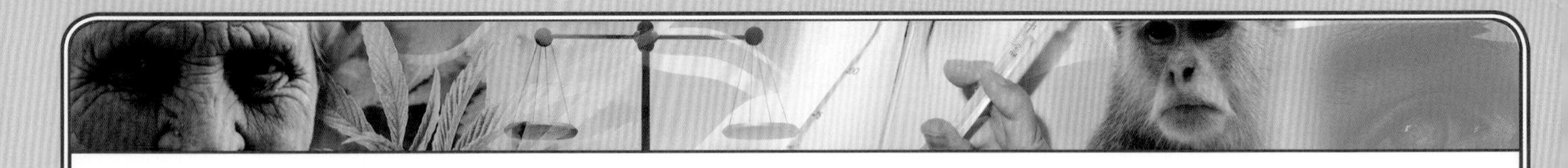

Young people aspire to be entrepreneurs

Interest in business is high among young people.

A lack of jobs and higher university tuition fees have led to a growing number of teenagers and young people aspiring to be their own boss, research finds.

According to a study of 1,000 young respondents by PC World Business, nearly half (44 per cent) are looking to set up their own business, with four-fifths of 16-year-olds reporting that they have had a business idea.

Some 44 per cent claim they could run their whole business using just a laptop.

Almost half of those surveyed are aiming to set up on their own in the next two years and an ambitious 19 per cent are looking to set up their business in the next six months.

According to a study of 1,000 young respondents by PC World Business, nearly half (44 per cent) are looking to set up their own business

Celebrity business programmes, such as *The Apprentice* and *Dragon's Den*, are influencing this group of young business stars, with nearly half (49 per cent) claiming they are more aware of entrepreneurial career options after watching business TV programmes.

Jamie Murray Wells, founder of Glasses Direct, says, 'As someone who started a business while at university, I am a big believer in helping those people with the drive, knowledge and business ideas to set up on their own.'

Even though more young people are looking to start a business, the research finds that there are barriers to setting up on your own. When asked what is stopping them from setting up their own business, 42 per cent claim lack of funding is the biggest hurdle and 29 per cent say they do not know where to start.

However, they were aware of the resources available to help them with their business, with 40 per cent saying they would use the Internet for advice, followed closely by mum and dad (38 per cent) and the bank (29 per cent).

7 September 2011

SMALLBUSINESS.CO.UK / FEDERATION OF SMALL BUSINESSES

Small business statistics

Information from the Federation of Small Businesses.

- There are 4.5 million small businesses in the UK.
- SMEs account for 99 per cent of all enterprise in the UK, 58.8 per cent of private sector employment and 48.8 per cent of private sector turnover.
- SMEs employed an estimated 13.8 million people and had an estimated combined annual turnover of £1,500 billion.
- Businesses with employees account for a quarter of all enterprises – a fall of 29,000 since 2010.
- There are 876,000 businesses in construction – a fifth of all UK enterprises.
- London has 748,000 enterprises – more than any other region.
- The South East has the second largest number of enterprises with 745,000. Combined with London, a third of all businesses are based here.
- 45.3 per cent of businesses are registered for VAT and/or PAYE.
- The number of sole proprietorships increased by 87,000 in 2010 and the number of companies, 6,000.

Micro: 0–9 employees. Small: 10–50 employees. Medium: 50–249 employees.

Figures obtained from the Department for Business, Innovation and Skills. Home working figures courtesy of Enterprise Nation.

Updated November 2011

PM challenges potential entrepreneurs to unleash the 'Business in You'

Cameron also pledges under-used government offices to start-ups.

The Prime Minister David Cameron has today unveiled a major campaign to boost entrepreneurship in the UK, following last week's reports that he would launch a new start-up initiative.

The nationwide 'Business in You' campaign – which was launched in partnership with StartUp Britain – aims to inspire potential entrepreneurs to start their own businesses and to encourage existing small businesses to grow.

Based on the concept that there is 'a business in everyone', the campaign will champion the stories of nine inspirational UK entrepreneurs, from a variety of backgrounds, who have used their passion or talent to develop successful businesses.

The ambassadors include Jamal Edwards, the 21-year-old founder of SBTV – an innovative broadcast company which has amassed more than 50 million YouTube views.

Moonfruit's Wendy Tan-White, Alastair Mitchell of Huddle, Richard Moross from moo.com and Paul Lindley, founder of Ella's Kitchen – one of the ten fastest-growing private companies in the UK – are also among the campaign heroes.

Cameron further pledged to make up to 300 empty and under-used government offices available to entrepreneurs struggling to find suitably flexible and affordable work spaces from which to start or grow their businesses.

Launching the campaign in front of an audience in Leeds this morning, Cameron said:

'Small businesses and entrepreneurs are the lifeblood of the British economy and I am determined that we, working with the private sector, do everything we can to help them to start up and to grow in 2012.

'I want to encourage people to go for it and make this the year of enterprise – whether that is fulfilling their dream of starting a new business or taking the leap to grow their business, to employ more staff, or to start exporting.'

The initiative will draw on the resources of a number of private sector partners to offer potential entrepreneurs advice on starting up, including workshops, web-based seminars and video tutorials, covering topics such as finding finance and mentors.

Michael Hayman, co-founder of StartUp Britain, added: 'Is there a business inside you? We believe the answer is yes and we want to inspire those with a dream to make it a reality by starting their own business.

'All around the country are people proving that you can make it in Britain, be your own boss and create the jobs that can help transform communities. This campaign champions the courage and determination of Britain's entrepreneurs – the people that change things. The people that have a go.'

23 January 2012

⇨ The above information is reprinted with kind permission from startups. Visit www.startups.co.uk for more information.

STARTUPS

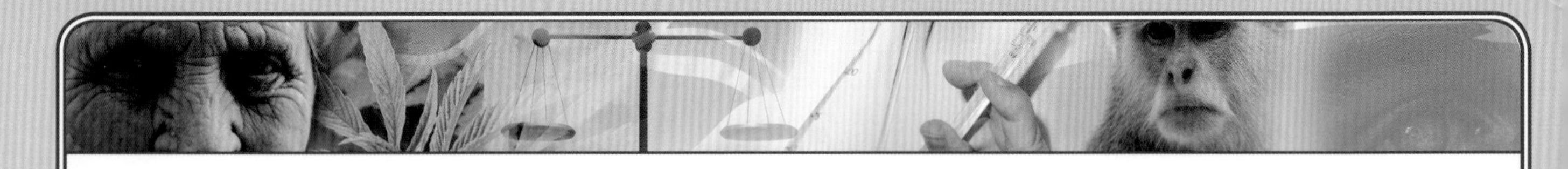

UK entrepreneurial spirit under pressure

Information from Aviva.

- Latest Aviva SME Pulse reveals one in four SME owners are considering returning to the workforce as an employee.
- A third say they have lost the enthusiasm to run their own business.
- Half say there has been a decline in the money drawn from their business for personal use over the past two years.

A significant proportion of small and medium-sized business owners are losing their entrepreneurial drive and thinking of returning to work, with 50% saying it is too tough to be a business owner in the current climate, according to the latest bi-annual SME Pulse from Aviva.

A quarter (26%) of SME owners admit they no longer enjoy running their business, with a third (32%) stating that they have lost the enthusiasm they had when they started their venture up. And as a result, the SME Pulse also reveals that one in four (25%) SME owners are considering returning to the workforce as an employee.

A reduction in the money they take out of their own businesses for personal use may be a contributing factor: half of those (50%) surveyed have reduced the money they draw over the past two years, with restaurant owners suffering the biggest fall. Nearly three-quarters (73%) of those with businesses in the catering sector have seen a marked decline in the amount they withdraw from their business – with almost a third (29%) reporting a drop of between 20–25% and 10% reporting a drop of up to 50%.

SMEs facing challenging economic times

Aviva's SME Pulse continues to track economic sentiment among business owners and the survey reveals that SMEs experienced a tough end to 2011. Nearly half (43%) said 2011 was tougher than expected, an increase since June 2011 when over one-third (37%) expressed this opinion. This sentiment was particularly prevalent among independent retailers and shop keepers with half of those questioned (50%) saying 2011 was tougher than expected; the highest of any other business type surveyed.

AVIVA

Looking to 2012, there appears to be little improvement in sentiment. More than one in three (35%) believes there is an increasing risk of an economic 'double dip' recession, a further increase compared with 28% when we asked the same question in the last Aviva SME research in June 2011.

A quarter of businesses (26%) expect the first half of the year to be difficult as people curb their spending, with 24% of those surveyed expecting a decline in sales. Less than one in ten (7%) expect good sales in the first six months this year.

David Bruce, commercial product manager at Aviva, comments: 'The mood continues to be downbeat about the economy as 2012 begins. Businesses are struggling against a backdrop of consumers' spending cuts and many don't envisage an improvement to the situation in the next six months.

'In addition, half of the SMEs we surveyed said they had not asked for funds from their bank, with the same number telling us they had reduced the money they took from their business, suggesting businesses may be "self-funding" their activities. This could be forcing them to focus more on the day-to-day operations than on planning for the future.

'Entrepreneurship is fundamental to economic growth – the Government last year called for a private-sector-led recovery to help stimulate growth and yet, our research shows that the entrepreneurial spirit is being challenged, with a significant number of owners thinking about returning to the workforce.'

24 January 2012

➪ The above information is an extract from Aviva's press release *UK entrepreneurial spirit under pressure* and is reprinted with their kind permission. Visit www.aviva.com for more information or to view the full text.

Chapter 2 CORPORATE RESPONSIBILITY

Corporate social responsibility

Information from tutor2u.

Definitions of social responsibility

Corporate social responsibility (CSR) is:

- An obligation, beyond that required by the law and economics, for a firm to pursue long-term goals that are good for society.
- The continuing commitment by business to behave ethically and contribute to economic development while improving the quality of life of the workforce and their families as well as that of the local community and society at large.
- About how a company manages its business process to produce an overall positive impact on society.

Corporate social responsibility means:

- Conducting business in an ethical way and in the interests of the wider community.
- Responding positively to emerging societal priorities and expectations.
- A willingness to act ahead of regulatory confrontation.
- Balancing shareholder interests against the interests of the wider community.
- Being a good citizen in the community.

Is CSR the same as business ethics?

- There is clearly an overlap between CSR and business ethics.
- Both concepts concern values, objectives and decisions based on something other than the pursuit of profits.
- And socially responsible firms must act ethically.

The difference is that ethics concern individual actions which can be assessed as right or wrong by reference to moral principles.

CSR is about the organisation's obligations to all stakeholders – and not just shareholders.

There are four dimensions of corporate responsibility:

- Economic – responsibility to earn profit for owners.
- Legal – responsibility to comply with the law (society's codification of right and wrong).
- Ethical – not acting only for profit but doing what is right, just and fair.
- Voluntary and philanthropic – promoting human welfare and goodwill.
- Being a good corporate citizen contributing to the community and quality of life.

The debate on social responsibility

Not all business organisations behave in a socially responsible manner.

There are people who would argue that it is not the job of business organisations to be concerned about social issues and problems.

There are two schools of thought on this issue:

- In the free market view, the job of business is to create wealth with the interests of the shareholders as the guiding principle.
- The corporate social responsibility view is that business organisation should be concerned with social issues.

Free market view – a summary

- The role of business is to create wealth by providing goods and services.
- 'There is one and only one social responsibility of business – to use its resources and engage in activities designed to increase its profit so long as it stays within the rules of the game, which is to say, engages in open and free competition, without deception or fraud.' *Milton Friedman, American economist*
- Giving money away is like a self-imposed tax.
- Managers who have been put in charge of a business have no right to give away the money of the owners.
- Managers are employed to generate wealth for the shareholders – not give it away.
- Free markets and capitalism have been at the centre of economic and social development.

TUTOR2U

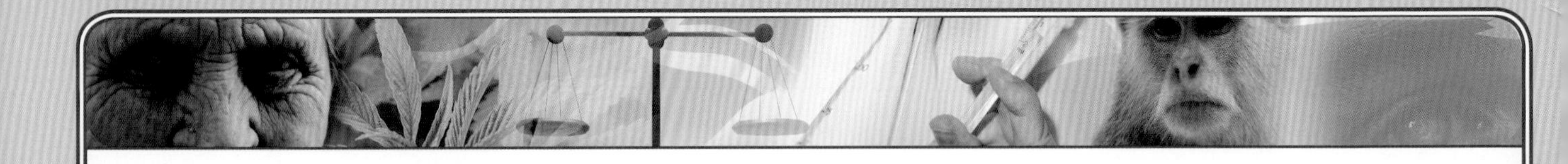

- Improvements in health and longevity have been made possible by economies driven by the free market.
- To attract quality workers it is necessary to offer better pay and conditions and this leads to a rise in standards of living and wealth creation.
- Free markets contribute to the effective management of scarce resources.
- It is true that at times the market fails and therefore some regulation is necessary to redress the balance.
- But the correcting of market failures is a matter for government – not business.
- Regulation should be kept to a minimum since regulation stifles initiative and creates a barrier to market entry.

The free market case against corporate social responsibility

- The only social responsibility of business is to create shareholder wealth.
- The efficient use of resources will be reduced if businesses are restricted in how they can produce.
- The pursuit of social goals dilutes business's primary purpose.
- Corporate management cannot decide what is in the social interest.
- Costs will be passed on to consumers.
- It reduces economic efficiency and profit.
- Directors have a legal obligation to manage the company in the interest of shareholders – and not for other stakeholders.
- CSR behaviour imposes additional costs which reduce competitiveness.
- CSR places unwelcome responsibilities on businesses rather than on government or individuals.

The corporate responsibility view

- Businesses do not have an unquestioned right to operate in society.
- Those managing business should recognise that they depend on society.
- Business relies on inputs from society and on socially-created institutions.
- There is a social contract between business and society, involving mutual obligations that society and business recognise that they have to each other.

Stakeholder theory

The basic premise is that business organisations have responsibility to various groups in society (the internal and external stakeholders) and not just the owners/ shareholders.

The responsibility includes a responsibility for the natural environment.

Decisions should be taken in the wider interest and not just the narrow shareholder interest.

Arguments for socially-responsible behaviour

- It is the ethical thing to do.
- It improves the firm's public image.
- It is necessary in order to avoid excessive regulation.
- Socially-responsible actions can be profitable.
- Improved social environment will be beneficial to the firm.
- It will be attractive to some investors.
- It can increase employee motivation.
- It helps to correct social problems caused by business.

Enlightened self-interest

This is the practice of acting in a way that is costly and/ or inconvenient at present but which is believed to be in one's best long-term interests.

There is a long history of philanthropy based on enlightened self-interests, e.g. Robert Owen's New Lanark Mills, Titus Salt's Saltaire as well the work of the Quaker chocolate makers such as Cadbury at Bournville and Rowntree in York.

Enlightened self-interest is summed up in this quotation from Anita Roddick (founder of The Body Shop): 'Being good is good for business'.

CSR behaviour can benefit the firm in several ways

- It aids the attraction and retention of staff.
- It attracts green and ethical investment.
- It attracts ethically-conscious customers.
- It can lead to a reduction in costs through recycling.
- It differentiates the firm from its competitor and can be a source of competitive advantage.
- It can lead to increased profitability in the long run.

TUTOR2U

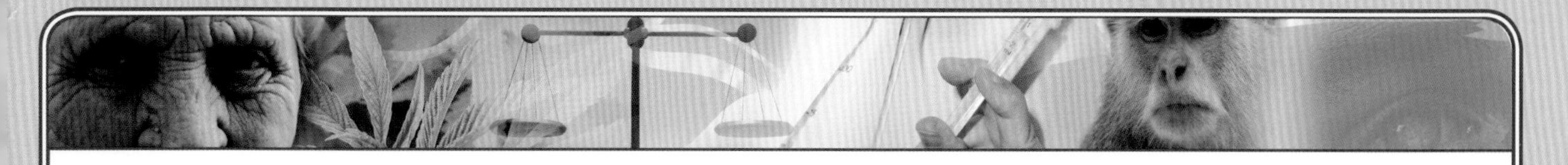

Surveys on business ethics, 2011

This article looks at the findings of selected surveys on business ethics issues published and carried out in 2011.

Every year the IBE commissions Ipsos MORI to survey the British public on their attitudes to ethics in business. The latest survey of three questions was conducted through face-to-face interviews in August 2011 among a representative sample of 1,001 British adults (aged 16 years and above).[1]

Q1. 'How ethically do you think British business generally behaves?'

Nearly six in ten, 58%, of the British public believe business behaves very (4%) or fairly (54%) ethically, a similar proportion to 2010 (59%) and one of the highest figures on record since the survey began in 2003. More 35- to 54-year-olds say they think business is behaving ethically (66%) whilst those aged 55+ years are less likely to say so (52%). Similar to the 35 to 54 age group, high proportions of people with children (63%) and those in employment (62%) also thought business behaves ethically.

Q2. 'How do you think British business is behaving now compared with ten years ago?'

The IBE & Ipsos MORI survey also examines attitudes towards ethics in business over time. The most common view is that British business behaves less ethically now than ten years ago (29% selected this option, a rise of nine percentage points this year compared to the 2010 figure). A similar proportion (28%) of people think British business is behaving more ethically than ten years ago. This is a decline of ten percentage points from 2010. The proportion thinking that British business is behaving the same now as ten years ago stands at 30%, similar to the 27% seen in 2010. The results for subgroups of the population follow a similar trend to question one. Those with children (36%), 35- to 54-year-olds (35%) and people in employment (32%) are most likely to think business is behaving more ethically now than ten years ago. Those aged 55+ are more likely to think business is behaving less ethically now than ten years ago (39%) compared to other subgroups.

Q3. 'In your view of company behaviour, which two or three of these issues most need addressing?'

As with previous years, the survey asked people to identify from a list the two or three issues they think most need addressing by business. 'Executive pay' was most commonly identified as an issue that needs addressing by the British public (36%), as has been the case since 2008. 'Discrimination in treatment of people' and 'Employees being able to speak out about company wrongdoing' were jointly the next most mentioned issues, each selected by 21% of respondents. These were closely followed by 'Environmental responsibility' and 'Bribery and corruption', selected by 20% and 19% of respondents, respectively. This contrasts to 2010 when 'Bribery and corruption' was the second least mentioned issue, with only 11% of respondents considering it an issue that needs to be addressed. 'Openness with information' rose by four percentage points, from 14% to 18%, making it the sixth issue most in need of addressing (in 2010 it was the tenth). 'Sweatshop labour' fell from being the third most mentioned issue (by 23% of the public) in 2010 to the eighth most mentioned (by 17%) in 2011.

Nearly six in ten, 58%, of the British public believe business behaves very (4%) or fairly (54%) ethically

There are some significant differences between subgroups of the population over which issues are most in need of addressing. For the issue 'Discrimination in treatment of people' there was a significant variation of 13 percentage points between the 16 to 34 (28%) and 55+ (15%) age groups. 'Harassment and bullying in the workplace' was identified as an important issue by 21% of women but only 15% of men. Similar disparity arose over 'Executive pay' – 39% of men and 33% of women thought it was an issue that needs addressing by business.

Note

1 A nationally representative quota sample of 1,001 British adults aged 16+ were interviewed throughout Great Britain using the Ipsos MORI Capibus across 156 sampling points. Interviewing was conducted by CAPI (Computer Assisted Personal Interviewing), face-to-face in respondents' homes between 19 and 25 August 2011. Complete findings at http://www.ibe.org.uk/index.asp?upid=68&msid=12

⇨ The above information is reprinted with kind permission from the Institute of Business Ethics. Visit www.ibe.org.uk for more information.

INSTITUTE OF BUSINESS ETHICS

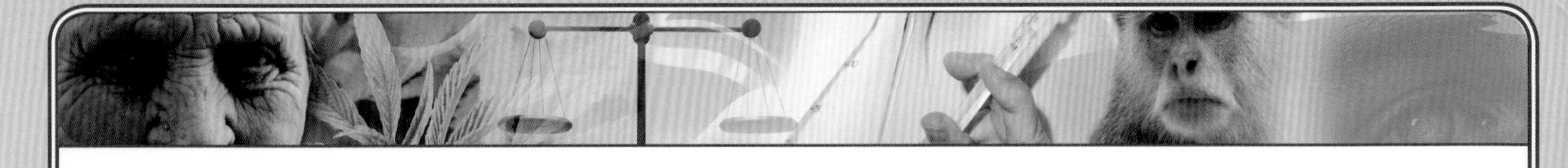

A world in trust

Leadership and corporate responsibility – significant quotes. Based on the global leadership study by Echo Research.

'The case against CSR: healthier foods, energy conservation and more fuel-efficient vehicles didn't become common until they became profitable ... The only sure way to influence corporate decision-making is to impose an unacceptable cost – regulatory mandates, taxes, punitive fines, public embarrassment – on socially unacceptable behaviour. Pleas for CSR will be truly embraced only by those executives who are smart enough to see that doing the right thing is a by-product of their pursuit of profit. And that renders such pleas pointless.'

Dr Aneel Karnani, Wall Street Journal

'It's clear we need a better way to evaluate business leaders. Moving forward, it appears that the new metric of corporate leadership will be closer to this: the extent to which executives create organisations that are economically, ethically and socially sustainable.'

James O'Toole and Warren Bennis

'Companies can show they are in touch with the real world and public concerns around fair play by looking long and hard at pay and incentive structures ... Core values are ... meaningless unless brought to life in performance reviews, reward and incentive structures, and confidential "whistle blowing" hotlines ... Businesses cannot always expect the public to like what they do, but they can and must work harder to ensure their actions are understood.'

Catherine May, Group Corporate Affairs Director, Centrica

'Institutions must prepare to move away from their traditional investor-led, one-way method of communication via dense and complex reports. All businesses should prepare for a sea-change in which they build and sustain an open and honest dialogue with the public.'

Philippa Foster Back, Director, Institute of Business Ethics

'In a growing number of companies CSR comes close to being embedded in the business, influencing decisions on everything from sourcing to strategy. These may also be the places where talented people will most want to work. The more this happens, ironically, the more the days of CSR may start to seem numbered. In time it will simply be the way business is done in the 21st century. "My job is to design myself out of a job," says one company's head of corporate responsibility.'

The Economist

'Driven by a combination of social conscience and economic pragmatism, Gaia capitalists are the early adopters of a "paradigm shift" questioning our understanding of what capitalism is for. They espouse a new form of it that factors in the environment and social wellbeing as a cost. It considers protecting the environment not only as a moral issue but as a set of design challenges to correct inefficiencies that make the capitalist system unsustainable. Waste, for example, is considered the result of inadequate thinking.'

Jessica Brinton, Sunday Times

'Leaders need deep-seated personal beliefs and values allied to considerable management skills.'

Ross Tieman, Financial Times

➪ The above information is an extract from Echo Research and International Business Leaders Forum's report *A World in Trust – Leadership and Corporate Responsibility*, and is reprinted with permission. Visit www.echoresearch.com for more information.

Business is a force for good, says British public

The BCC launches its campaign 'Business is Good for Britain'.

A survey of more than 2,000 members of the British public shows the overwhelming majority of people believe that businesses are 'good' for Britain as long as they comply with the law, pay their taxes, and make a profit (82%).

The findings, from a survey carried out by ComRes for the British Chambers of Commerce (BCC), also show that a majority of Britons believe local businesses play an important role in local communities (73%). Nearly half (46%) believe new or international companies will generate economic growth here in the UK, compared to only 20% saying this will come from government. It also shows they are not particularly optimistic about the future. Only 14% think the economy will improve in the next 12 months, and the majority (67%) believe unemployment will get worse.

The research is part of the business group's 'Business is Good for Britain' campaign, which is being launched today (1 February) in Central London. The campaign highlights the role of business as a positive force for the UK recovery, success of local communities and individuals.

How the public views business

- 82% of respondents believe businesses that comply with the law, pay their taxes and make a profit are good businesses (65% still believe this is the case no matter what sector they are in).
- 73% agreed that local businesses play an important role in their local community. Chambers of Commerce believe businesses are at the foundation of their local communities and help to create the wealth which allows them to thrive.
- More than two-thirds of those surveyed (72%) believe that a company's first priority should be their employees, while only 29% believe it should be to their owners and shareholders. This highlights tension between different business objectives, with the public clearly less favourable towards business profits than to provision of employment.
- Only 31% believe the public sector is better than the private sector at delivering economic growth and jobs, suggesting that most of the British public support the view that the private sector is the UK's real 'economic engine'.
- Worryingly, 59% agreed with the statement 'the UK is no longer a major trading nation'. In fact, the UK is the world's third largest exporter of services and tenth largest exporter of manufactured goods.

82% of respondents believe businesses that comply with the law, pay their taxes and make a profit are good businesses

- The majority of people (54%) believe 'businesses make a fair contribution to supporting public services' – although for people aged between 18 and 34 this dips to 47%. This suggests younger people are more disillusioned with the business community.

BRITISH CHAMBERS OF COMMERCE

The public's prediction for economic growth and how they see business's future role

- 79% of respondents believe creating new jobs should be a high priority for UK firms, compared to generating a profit (43%).
- Nearly half (46%) said new companies and international companies will generate economic growth, while only 20% believed this would come from central government. This result suggests that future government actions must focus on supporting and empowering business growth.
- Only 14% of people expect the economy to improve over the course of 2012. This underscores the need to persevere with measures to stimulate business growth, while reducing the deficit.
- The majority expect unemployment to get worse (67%), with only 7% expecting improvement. This is in line with the BCC's latest economic forecast which predicts unemployment will reach 2.77 million by the end of this year.

Commenting on the findings, John Longworth, Director General of the British Chambers of Commerce (BCC), said:

'Businesses up and down the country are doing their utmost to find new markets and grow their firms, despite the difficult economic challenges they face. The British public is savvy and recognises that business is a force for good. They are the ones that live and work in business every day. But it is those in government, the policy-makers and the commentators that we need to convince.

'Business is at the centre of the economy, and only the private sector will drive recovery and help deliver public services, like education, healthcare and pensions. It is the foundation of local communities, creating the wealth that helps them thrive, providing hard-working people with purpose and self-respect, and employment and training for those that want to learn. More than two-thirds of people said the private sector is better at delivering growth than the public sector. While the public sector has a vital role to play, the private sector is our real economic engine.

'It is worrying though, that more than half said Britain is no longer a major trading nation. There are thousands of fantastic companies in this country, both in manufacturing and services that bust this myth. And there are thousands of others who have products ready for the export market, but they need support and encouragement to break into new markets and boost their orders overseas.

'The British public thinks job creation should be a high priority for UK businesses. But businesses can't do this alone. The Government must create the best possible environment to allow firms to grow. Cutting burdensome red tape and implementing its promised credit-easing measures would give companies the confidence they need to take on more staff.

'What's more, it is concerning that many members of the public seem to think that profit should not be one of business's top priorities. But without profits, businesses can't generate employment, pay more in tax, or expand into new markets. Profit and success are an essential part of enterprise and our future prospects.'

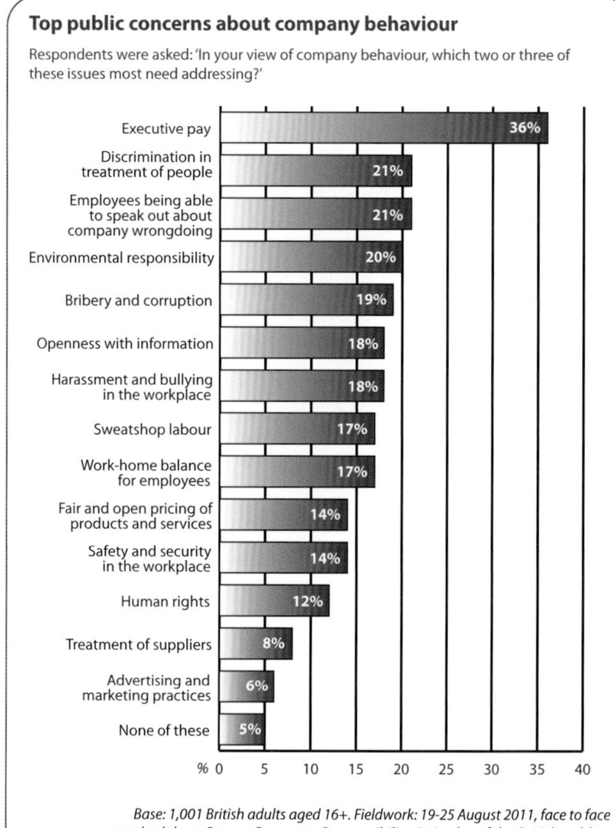

Base: 1,001 British adults aged 16+. Fieldwork: 19-25 August 2011, face to face methodology. Source: Corporate Responsibility Attitudes of the British public - Ethics in Business *(report for Institute of Business Ethics). Ipsos MORI.*

Commenting on the BCC's Business is Good for Britain campaign, Prime Minister David Cameron said:

'Britain's history is built on having some of the most innovative, dynamic and creative businesses in the world. Their success is crucial for this country's future so I want this to be the year we really get behind them, with more people starting and growing their businesses. They are the engines of new job creation and economic growth that this country depends upon.'

1 February 2012

- The above information is reprinted with kind permission from British Chambers of Commerce. Visit www.britishchambers.org.uk for more information.

Anti-business?

Information from the Trades Union Congress (TUC).

By Kevin Rowan, Regional Secretary, Northern TUC

The predictable outcry from some of the dimmer lights in the world of business against the voices expressing concern about excessive bonus payments are nothing more than a wafer-thin defence of corporate greed that has been growing for 30 years or more. The 'moral' shock that was associated with Fred Goodwin being un-knighted was not only so completely contra to the general public attitude towards the cabal of wealthy banking executives that got us all into the economic mess that we're in, it is also a further demonstration of the sheer lack of any contrition for the damage that they have done.

Anyone who now suggests that multi-million pound bonuses on top of multi-million pound salaries are wrong is accused of 'business bashing'

Anyone who now suggests that multi-million pound bonuses on top of multi-million pound salaries are wrong is accused of 'business bashing', while the Chancellor is apparently worried that these challenges to the stupendously crass demonstrations of deep-rooted and extreme unfairness might actually harm business. This is despite the obvious and ongoing experience of workers at the bottom and in the middle of the labour market of paying for the follies of this 'super-executive' breed with their jobs, their livelihoods and their homes. Somehow, despite struggling to survive in these most difficult circumstances, the vast majority are expected to placidly witness the continued unjustified platinum-plating of the extremely well-off's wage packets.

This is a long-term trend. In 1978, 58 per cent of the country's GDP was paid out in wages. In 2012 this is down to 53.4 per cent, and within that reduced share of wealth, the inequality between the top few very high earners and the mass majority of average- and low-paid workers has continued to grow. The average top salary in the FTSE 100 companies is about 300 times higher than the average salaries across those companies. As Richard Wilkinson, author of *The Spirit Level*, said in his public lecture at Newcastle University, what better way is there to show how little people are valued than by paying them 300 times less than yourself?

There is little wonder that there is a growing sense of fury about the boardroom excesses of a small number of over-paid, greedy corporate executives. Everywhere ordinary people turn there is experience of hardship – people enduring pay freezes and cuts, increases in child poverty, people choosing between heating and eating, children being taken into care, families losing their homes. The only surprise is that people aren't more angry and that there isn't more protest and demonstration against this obvious inequity.

Proper rewards for success no-one should argue against. A fairer distribution of the benefits of that success would benefit everybody, especially if that results in pay rises for lower-paid workers, which are recycled into the economy in larger proportions than bonuses for the privileged few, leading to better longer-term economic outcomes. Squeezing the worst-off even more, while those at the top continue to take a bigger and bigger share of the wealth, can only lead to greater problems further down the line.

13 February 2012

⇨ The above information is reprinted with kind permission from the Trades Union Congress (TUC). Visit www.tuc.org.uk for more information.

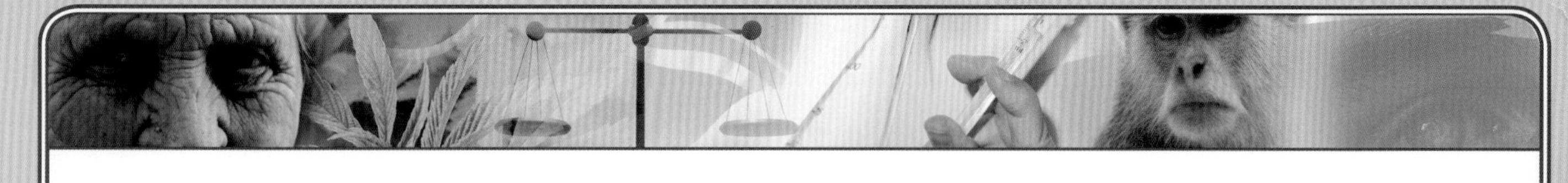

Key facts

Information from Occupy Bristol.

The super rich

- The top 1% earn £118,027 or more per year. (Source: BBC).
- In Bristol some of the top 1% are paid out of our council tax. (Source: *Bristol Evening Post*)
- In Bristol, many of the Merchant Venturers will be part of the 1%.
- The top 10% now have 100 times the wealth of the bottom 10%. (Source: *Hills Report*)
- The top 10% earn 4.1 times the incomes of the bottom 10%, with the top 1% earning more than ten times that of the bottom 10%. This figure was 3.1 in 1961.
- The average CEO earns 250 times more than the average cleaner.
- Levels of social mobility in the UK are the lowest among all developed economies.
- There are more than 50 hedge fund managers among Britain's richest 1,000 people. (Source: *Sunday Times* Rich List)

Bank bail-outs

The Bank of England estimates that the total cost of bailing out the financial system is £1.3 trillion, or more than ten times the entire NHS budget. The UK bank bailout accounts for about one-third of the global banking bailout.

Three years on, the British Government continues to subsidise 'too-big-to-fail' banks:

- £46 billion: the combined subsidy the 'Big Five' UK banks enjoyed in 2010;
- £10 billion: British taxpayers' money paid in indirect subsidy to Barclays;
- Lloyds, RBS, HSBC and Nationwide also enjoyed subsidies of £15 billion, £13 billion, £7 billion and £1 billion respectively.

The 'too-big-to-fail' subsidy for the UK's largest four banks is 62% higher than the equivalent subsidy in Germany, despite the fact that the German economy is significantly larger.

New Economics Foundation, Quid Pro Quo*, September 2011*

Austerity cuts

£83 billion: the amount of public sector cuts planned by the Government by 2014-15, effectively cutting the incomes of ordinary people by:

- 6.2% for typical families with two young people on modest earnings (£37,000 combined income);
- 4.2% for more well-off families with children at university (£78,000 combined income);
- 10.4% for the average working lone parent with two children;
- 16.2% for pensioner couples.

The cuts are hitting the poorest hardest, according to the Institute for Fiscal Studies.

TUC, Where the Money Goes*, October 2010*

Unemployment

- The economy has lost two million jobs since the beginning of the recession.
- 2.57 million people are out of work (or 8.1% of the working-age population).
- 21.3% of 16- to 25-year-olds are out of work. That is almost one million young people, the demographic group that has lost out most from the fall in demand for labour.
- 250,000 jobs have been cut in the public sector in the last year.
- Research published by TUC found that those previously working in the lowest-paid jobs make up nearly half of all new unemployed claimants since 2008.

➪ The above information is reprinted with kind permission from Occupy Bristol. Visit www.occupybristoluk.org for more.

OCCUPY BRISTOL

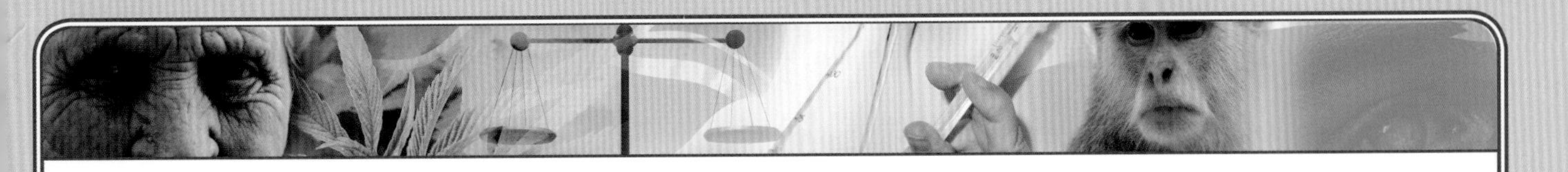

In an age of austerity, can capitalism really be popular?

When even David Cameron has his doubts, backing business is a thankless task.

Banging the drum for British business can be a thankless job at the best of times; but now, as politicians across the spectrum vie to offer searing critiques of capitalism, it's hardly surprising many firms feel unloved. In London this week, a new campaign will be launched, aimed at persuading the recession-scarred public that 'Business is Good for Britain'.

John Longworth, Director-General of the British Chambers of Commerce (BCC), which came up with the idea, is keen to separate his members – typically smaller companies – from the bonus-wielding City fat cats and boardroom bosses whose behaviour so infuriates the public.

'These are businesses that are civically minded; they're businesses that are part of the local community; they care about what they're doing,' he says. 'They're passionate about creating wealth and jobs, and doing the right thing.'

And it is creating jobs that most of the British public regard as the main responsibility of business, judging by a survey carried out by polling group ComRes for the BCC. More than two-thirds (72%) of the 2,000 people surveyed thought that a company's first priority should be to its workforce; less than a third said its shareholders should come first. 'We have got to get business-focused in the UK,' Longworth says.

But the problem for him and his members is that at a time when falling living standards and rising unemployment are making life hard, many of the public have come to associate business with the get-rich-quick 'predators' attacked by Labour leader Ed Miliband in his party conference speech last autumn; and even Cameron has admitted that something has gone awry.

Chuka Umunna, Labour's Shadow Business Secretary, says: 'I'm extremely worried that business is being depicted as being in the naughty corner. Business relies on society to provide the talent and skills they need, and society relies on business to create wealth and prosperity.'

Andrew Cave, spokesman for the Federation of Small Businesses, says many smaller firms would agree with the argument that something has gone wrong with the system.

'Our members are the victims of many of the practices that are now being picked on by politicians,' he says. Small British firms – with an average of four employees – often remain small: 'There's a very strong argument to get back to the kind of capitalism that allows companies to grow from the smallest businesses to the biggest.'

More than two-thirds (72%) of the 2,000 people surveyed thought that a company's first priority should be to its workforce; less than a third said its shareholders should come first

British entrepreneurs tend to expand their firm to a certain size and then sell out, often to an overseas investor – or, in more recent years, a private equity house. So Cave says one of the things that may need a rethink is the Government's role in nurturing the growth of firms. The Department for Business, Innovation and Skills, and its predecessor, the DTI, have traditionally taken a hands-off, laissez-faire approach, championing foreign investment and deregulation; but even in the US, cradle of no-holds-barred capitalism, the Government has often intervened to block takeovers and champion domestic firms.

President Obama has proudly cited the resurgence of American carmakers GM and Chrysler, which were bailed out by Congress at the height of the credit crisis, but have since bounced back.

'When you actually go to the States, there's a huge amount of protectionism: it stems from a pride in having a business that grows out of its local community, and has roots in its community,' says Cave.

Under Lord Mandelson, and now Vince Cable, the Department for Business has tried to take a more activist approach, and the Government's new Enterprise Zones are meant to encourage business expansion, by granting tax breaks to firms that create jobs. But with corporate tax avoidance, bumper bonuses and rising unemployment hitting the headlines, teaching Britain to love business will be a hard sell.

➪ This article first appeared in *The Observer*, 29 January 2012

THE OBSERVER

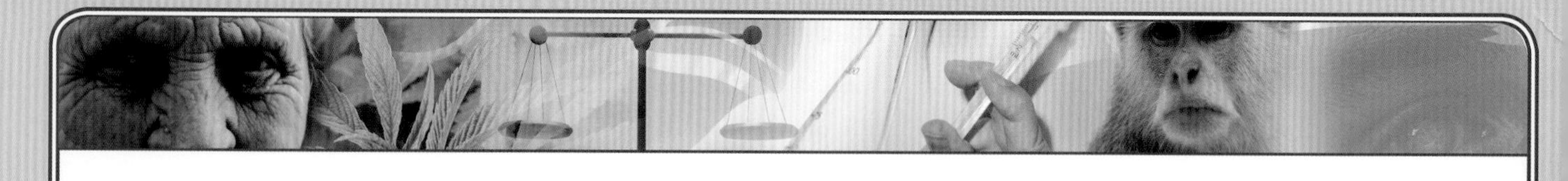

Mind your own business

The corporate world must put its own house in order.

By Patience Wheatcroft

Who will rescue capitalism? As the voices of its critics grow louder, those of us who would defend the moneymakers must not be cowed. But even the most ardent supporters of the profit motive would probably concede that capitalism has been veering in the wrong direction, providing sufficient ammunition for its detractors to raise doubts over the sustainability of the system itself. With public anger over bankers in particular, and 'fat cats' in general, politicians – of all parties – have seen an opportunity to empathise with demonstrators' banners and the shrieking from the media.

Warm, even occasionally wise, words have flowed, defining how capitalism should be. David Cameron wants it to be 'fair'; Ed Miliband wants it to be 'responsible'; and Nick Clegg favours the John Lewis variety. All admirable sentiments, but just try legislating for such ideals – let alone policing them. That is why, after almost every minister and backbencher has had their say, all that is promised is tougher rules on transparency of boardroom pay and yet another look at empowering shareholders.

Even Vince Cable's much-hyped proposals have been greeted with relative sanguinity by business. Calls for more transparency are themselves easily seen through: enough information is already available for the High Pay Commission to report that, in the past decade, the average remuneration of a FTSE 100 chief executive rose from 69 times that of the average worker to 145 times. The ensuing publicity did nothing to halt a trend which is now set to take the ratio to 214 times over the next ten years. Giving more power to shareholders is unlikely to produce a speedy change. The institutional investors who own most of corporate Britain demonstrate pitifully little enthusiasm for engaging in such issues.

In my time as a City editor, I found that I became far more exercised about what was going on within companies than those who actually owned the companies. If shareholders were unhappy or concerned, they would simply sell the stock. Too often – if they were happy and the stock had risen – they would still sell the stock. Little wonder that the directors who sit on the boards of corporate Britain have limited respect for those whom, in theory, they serve. Those of us keen to save the reputation of capitalism should not invest too much hope in these 'absentee owners'.

Perhaps more hope lies in those who have been enjoying the rich rewards, and who should realise that their position is looking increasingly precarious. The West may have deemed capitalism the best system in the past, but if it is seen to be failing the majority of the people, they will reach for alternatives. The clamour to rein in free markets will grow until politicians acknowledge that mere words will not be enough to quell it.

If a political backlash is to be avoided, then business must put its own house in order. At the end of last year David Jones, a man dubbed an 'advertising guru' and a former adviser to Cameron, published a book entitled *Who Cares Wins: Why Good Business is Better Business*. It is a treatise in praise of what was once labelled Corporate Social Responsibility, something of which, at its box-ticking worst, I was once roundly scathing. But while I remain suspicious about much of this agenda, with its emphasis on diversity quotients and pious mission statements, I am convinced that business needs to look beyond the bottom line.

Commerce has to be seen as a force for good, not merely a generator of fat salaries for the people at the top. That starts by producing the goods or services that people are willing, and want, to purchase, but it must go further. I became a David Cameron fan in his pre-Big Society days, when he first talked about the need to fix the 'broken society'. The scale of the task is daunting, and few would question the fact that it is a problem that government alone cannot fix. Business can, and should, play a major role.

Adam Smith, that great respecter of the profit motive, was suspicious about the idea of ethical business:

THE SPECTATOR

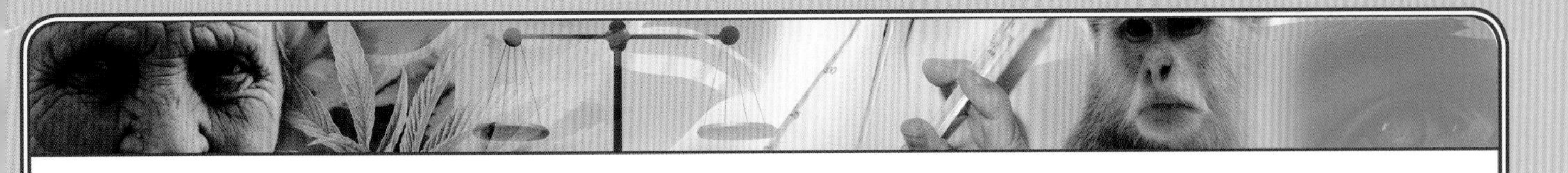

'I have never known much good done by those who affected to trade for the public good,' he wrote. But his invisible hand would align the concerns of business and society. Fixing broken Britain would not reflect any sense of corporate altruism, but an understanding that business can flourish best in a society which is thriving, well-educated and law-abiding.

And this agenda is under way. There are already plenty of examples of companies making a difference, whether it be taking ex-offenders into employment, or providing work experience and mentoring for children who might otherwise be disaffected truants (and graduate into disaffected, unemployed adults). Just as the Victorians gave us the corporate towns, places such as Bournville, Cadbury's chocolate box suburb, and Port Sunlight, a bricks-and-mortar tribute to Unilever's washing powder. Without being so proprietorial, modern business could have a big and positive impact on communities. Nike, for instance, decided that its brand was at risk of contamination over allegations that it used child labour. Its response was to donate basketball courts to numerous communities, a move that goes on scoring positively for the brand, keeping youths healthily engaged and, perhaps, buying rather than looting their trainers.

Major companies are currently hoarding large piles of cash, too nervous of what economic shocks lie around the corner to invest in hefty acquisitions or new projects. Putting a small proportion of this saving into an infant business or social enterprise could make a huge difference, where conventional bank funding is failing. Add some management mentoring, and the equation looks even better.

Non-executive directors are not all the patsies they are painted as, although 'group think' can and does permeate many a boardroom. Now is the time they could really demonstrate their worth, becoming the crusaders for not merely fair but creative capitalism. Bringing a sense of proportion to remuneration would just be one step on the way.

It is clear, even to hardened free-marketeers like myself, that things have to change. If they don't, we may all be bemoaning the death of capitalism. And I certainly don't relish the alternatives.

28 January 2012

⇨ Information from *The Spectator*. Visit www.spectator.co.uk for more.

We must still reward success, says Cridland

CBI Director-General tells* Evening Standard *that politicians' 'anti-business rhetoric' has increased as public frustration with the state of the economy has grown.

Politicians are using 'anti-business rhetoric' to chime with public frustration at the state of the economy – and large bonuses are justified if they are earned by excellent performance, the CBI Director-General has told the *Evening Standard.*

John Cridland reinforced his message that rewards should be given only where they are justified – comparing high-performing directors to top footballers.

'The whole football team knows that their performance requires one or two star players, and I think it's the same with a board of directors,' he said. 'That is why some payments will be high but they should only be high if they are for the equivalent of a goalscorer in the Premier League.'

Mr Cridland went on to identify politicians as contributing to the recent negative publicity around business.

He added: 'The anti-business rhetoric that we saw in the autumn at the three party conferences has increased since. I don't think it's an accident that it has increased as public nervousness at the state of the economy has increased. As people feel understandably worried about our economic prospects, politicians are looking for some way to characterise that frustration.'

The CBI chief also used the interview, published in today's *Evening Standard*, to give his view on the relationship between the CBI and the Government ('It's a working partnership'); the state of the economy ('There are just the beginnings of a sign that confidence may be rebuilding and exporters in particular may be feeling slightly better'); and the education system ('The lack of value added for under-performing 11-year-olds up to the age of 16 is a national scandal').

10 February 2012

⇨ The above information is reprinted with kind permission from the CBI. Visit www.cbi.org.uk for more information.

THE SPECTATOR / CBI

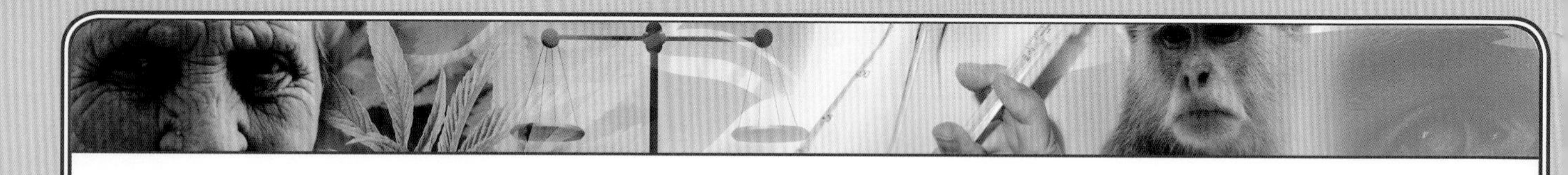

We need a New Philanthropy for the 21st century

In the aftermath of the credit crisis, it is easy to forget that business can be a powerful force for good.

By Sir Victor Blank, formerly Chairman of Lloyds Banking Group

'We make a living by what we get, but we make a life by what we give.'

That isn't the best known of Sir Winston Churchill's observations, but it is one of his most astute. His insight is even more relevant today as individuals and companies reflect on the financial crisis.

The credit crunch has provoked some deep soul-searching about money, debt, the pursuit of profit and the purpose of companies. Do businesses exist merely to maximise shareholder value, or do they have a wider responsibility to communities in which they operate?

Business leaders need to look back at the lessons to be learnt from the crisis, but we also need to look forward. In the wave of recriminations after the crunch, we are in danger of forgetting the fact that business can be a powerful force for good, not least through the power of philanthropy. Companies and individual business people already play a major role supporting charities carrying out valuable work in the UK and overseas.

After the credit crunch, we need their contribution more than ever before – a New Philanthropy for the 21st century – to help address the enormous challenges. These include the fight against poverty and disease, building a sustainable economic future in the face of climate change, and supporting those who are disadvantaged, disabled and even disaffected within our communities.

Governments can play a big part in solving some of these problems, but public finances in the UK and elsewhere will be under strain for years and we need the corporate sector to help. Businesses have a strong incentive to get involved, not just because of altruism or to rehabilitate themselves after the crunch, but because customers are demanding responsible corporate citizenship.

Philanthropy on its own will not – and should not – restore the damage to the reputation of banks or rebuild their moral capital: the scale of that task should not be underestimated. But, along with commitment to best business values, it has a part to play for companies wanting to regain the trust and respect of communities in which they operate.

THE DAILY TELEGRAPH

The UK has a proud heritage of socially aware capitalism. In the 19th century, Quaker business people including the Cadbury family, for example, were pioneers of corporate social responsibility, setting up decent housing for their workers. George Cadbury believed 'no man ought to be condemned to live in a place where a rose cannot grow'.

Do businesses exist merely to maximise shareholder value, or do they have a wider responsibility to communities in which they operate?

This was at a time when the Industrial Revolution had condemned thousands of workers to slum dwellings, ill health and the terror of the workhouse in old age.

By contrast, Bournville village, based on his vision of a 'factory in a garden', is still a desirable place to live today.

The world has changed enormously since then and Cadbury itself was recently taken over by US food manufacturer Kraft. Globalisation, outsourcing and the Internet can mean that the connections between businesses and local communities feel weaker, as employees and customers are scattered in far flung locations. We may feel nostalgic, but we cannot turn the clock back to a golden age of paternalistic capitalism, if one ever existed. The openness of the UK economy is one of its great strengths, encouraging foreign investment here and keeping down the cost of goods to UK consumers. These seismic changes, however, mean it is more important than ever for businesses to forge links with local communities.

Lloyds Banking Group, where I was chairman, funds four charitable foundations covering England and Wales, Scotland, Northern Ireland and the Channel Islands.

Their mission is to improve the lives of disadvantaged people in local communities. The foundations received £29 million last year, taking the total contributions since 1997 to more than £390 million, money that has made a huge difference to many people's lives. Some of the people helped by these programmes will get their lives on track, get jobs and start businesses.

The idea that there is a sharp divide between charity and commerce is false – the interests of a company and its customers are often synonymous. Avon, the door-to-door cosmetics company, for example, has a clear commercial interest in women's health and wellbeing. Its philanthropic foundation, set up in 1955 with a scholarship of $400, had by last year raised and awarded more than $725 million (£457 million) worldwide to improve women's lives. Its current focus is on breast cancer, domestic violence and women and families affected by disasters. Without the work of the Avon foundation, thousands of women worldwide, who are under-served medically and might have gone undiagnosed, have been given a better chance of surviving breast cancer.

Bill Gates, the founder of Microsoft, recently pledged £6 billion to develop and distribute vaccines which could save the lives of more than eight million children in the poorest countries

The charity Wellbeing of Women, which I chair, aims to improve the health and quality of life of all women. Its work on all aspects of reproductive health has benefited every woman and child in the UK. The quality of women's health has an impact on every company, benefiting its female employees and their families.

Philanthropy from the business world can make a huge difference to some of the most vulnerable people. Bill Gates, the founder of Microsoft, recently pledged £6 billion to develop and distribute vaccines which could save the lives of more than eight million children in the poorest countries. Even the most jaded observer would surely find it hard not to be heartened by generosity on that scale.

Others in the mega-rich category, such as Warren Buffett and Ted Turner, are also setting the lead, with many committing a very substantial portion of their wealth to benefit the poor and the diseased.

In the UK, businesses feel under pressure to save costs, but they should recognise charity not as an optional extra but as a core part of their responsibility.

Average annual charitable donations by a FTSE 100 company amount to something less than one-fifth of one per cent of profits. The figure should be a multiple of that and shareholders as well as corporate management should recognise the importance of using corporate resources to build a better, more balanced, more equal society.

But it is not just a question of money. One in four charities has seen donations fall, according to a survey by the Charities Commission last year. More than half had been affected by an increase in costs, and one in five experienced more demand for services, particularly those involving care for the elderly, health and social services.

Companies have a marvellous resource to share with charities: employees. Staff at all levels can bring skills, expertise and contacts into the charity world and go back to their desks with a new perspective on life.

As companies look to their future in a post-credit crunch era, perhaps it is time to rewrite the old proverb and adopt the motto that Charity Begins at Work.

Programmes of employee engagement, where companies make time available for their employees, combined with enhanced philanthropic giving, can make massive improvements to society and, ultimately, benefit the bottom line also.

There is an opportunity now to make a difference and business will reject this at its peril.

22 January 2011

THE DAILY TELEGRAPH

Why do good companies do bad things?

Simon Hodgson argues that conflating morality and the responsibilities of business isn't always helpful.

As David Cameron and Ed Miliband take turns to propose a newer moral form of capitalism, the question I've heard a hundred times from taxi drivers, dinner party guests and playground acquaintances is 'do they care?'. And I always hesitate, but tend to settle for 'it depends'.

It's an occupational hazard and the dialogue goes the same way: 'What do you do?'

'I'm a very specialised sort of management consultant.'

'Doing what?'

'Working with big companies on social, environmental and ethical issues.'

'Oh, interesting. Lots of call for that I'd imagine. And you must see the inside story – tell me, do they care?'

The problem is that before we can answer the question, we need to completely deconstruct it. Who's 'they'? And what do we mean by 'care'? The more I've thought it, the more convinced I've become that at best the question is a nonsense (what philosophers call a 'category error') and at worst it's holding society back from making progress on some of the biggest problems it faces.

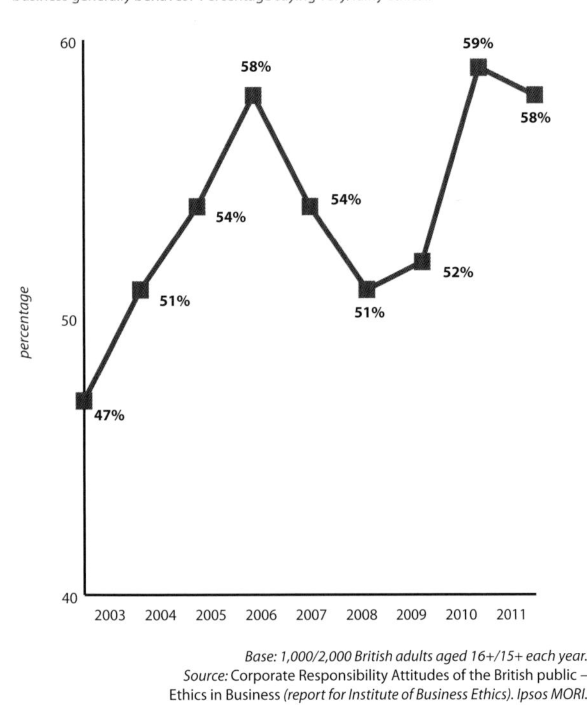

Because business does have a profound effect on the world around us and that effect is not always for good. From catalysing the credit crunch to the evidence before the Leveson enquiry. From carbon footprints to accusations of driving runaway consumption. From government lobbying to iniquitous bonuses. There is no shortage of material to paint businesses as psychopathic villains, with no values or morals.

Companies bring us food, water, clothes and shelter, mobile phones, gadgets and entertainment. And they are getting ever kinder as they do so

Step forward the alternative view. Companies bring us food, water, clothes and shelter, mobile phones, gadgets and entertainment. And they are getting ever kinder as they do so, with warm corporate values, inspiring vision statements, recycling policies, caring employment practices and mega-bucks charity cheques for smiling children.

The question we end up with is 'are companies nice or nasty?' There seems to be a battle going on for the soul of business.

But there are some grave problems with this framing. The most obvious is that the company isn't a moral entity. It's made up of thousands of people – some nice and some nasty – and (usually) paid for by thousands of shareholders. How can it possibly be said to have one set of values? How can it 'care'?

To solve this, we conflate the company with the people running it. So campaigners and the media focus on those running large companies, concluding that they are morally 'worse' than the rest of us. They do what they do because they are callous, greedy, indifferent or even psychopathic. If that's true, then it's only reasonable that we should control them. They must answer personally to the law at every turn. We should see who they meet for lunch and what they are paid.

But what if people running companies are morally no different from the rest of us? What if they are – on the whole – no greedier, no less caring about the environment, no less capable of feeling or empathy than anyone else?

THE GUARDIAN

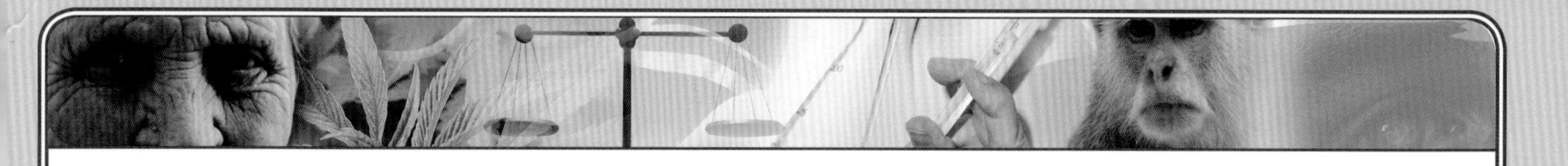

My experience is that this is much closer to reality. If we think this way it leads to a very different framing of the whole discussion on big business, society and the environment. If the people inside companies start off just like you and I and they are doing things that we wouldn't want them to do then we need to ask a very different set of questions. Why do they act as they do? Why do they put so much pressure on workers? Why do they seek political influence? Why do they damage the environment?

If it's more profitable for a company to legally dump its waste than treat it, we shouldn't wring our hands and say it's being naughty. It's doing exactly what one would expect given the way the market is set up

To answer questions put this way, we need to explore incentives, systems, market failures and regulations. And – I believe – it leads to a much more effective way of getting what we want: businesses that work in the interests of society, not against it.

Of course, business is partly to blame. It has certainly responded to accusations of moral failing with moral crusade. But those of us inside companies then find ourselves having to justify 'niceness' using a financial case. But in doing so we are mixing oil and water; making the argument for an ethical principle based on a financial argument. In the end, there's a deep reluctance in business to get drawn into the argument on a truly moral basis. And there is a similarly great frustration in society that business won't do this and instead reverts constantly back to profits.

So what do we do? I think we need to reframe the arguments about responsible business without reference to morals. Businesses certainly need to conform to the consensus moral standards of society. They mustn't lie, cheat or steal.

But beyond that we need to be a little more dispassionate. If it's more profitable for a company to legally dump its waste than treat it, we shouldn't wring our hands and say it's being naughty. It's doing exactly what one would expect given the way the market is set up. Change the rules. If no one in society wants to buy expensive, unreliable renewable technologies, we can't blame companies for not selling them. We need to encourage investment and development to the point at which they are must-have no-brainers. And if we want workers in the developing world to be paid better, we need to somehow connect the buyer of the iPhone with the hands that assemble it. Product provenance on the label. Change the rules.

These are major system changes, and need to be thought through thoroughly, to the minutest details. They still leave room for voluntarism. But, to use the phrase literally, if the 'bottom line' is social benefit, then a well-constructed market is one of the best ways to guarantee it.

Simon Hodgson is a senior partner at Acona

6 February 2012

THE GUARDIAN

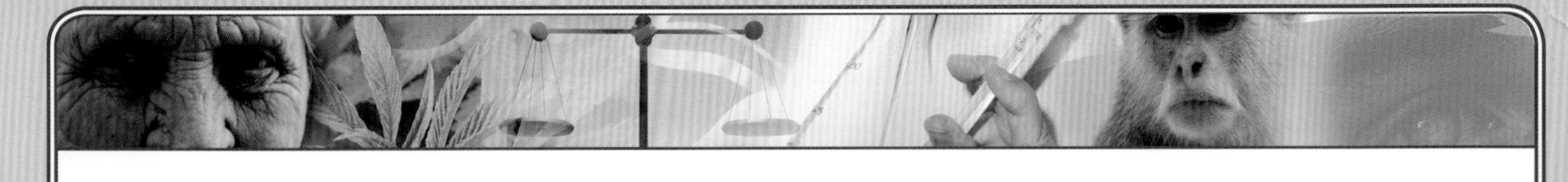

Just deserts, or good luck?

High earners' attitudes to pay.

Pay is a rarely discussed topic. In the UK it can be a social taboo to discuss your income or attitudes to your earnings, yet understanding what people earn and where we each sit in the pay hierarchy is an important part of understanding and engaging in our society. For this reason the High Pay Commission commissioned research to understand attitudes to pay. This report explores what top earners think about their pay. The research looked specifically at attitudes towards desert and luck; whether top earners understood where they sat in the income distribution; and whether they saw themselves as the 'squeezed middle' or felt that we were all 'in it together'.

This qualitative study of high earners looks at the attitudes of those in the top 1% of the income distribution, and revealed some important issues.

Do we get what we deserve?

- Many felt pay levels were determined by the market, by luck, and by ability to negotiate.

- For most participants, there was little correlation between hard work and/or aptitude and the absolute amount that a person earns.
- There was an acknowledgement that individual performance is usually hard to quantify in terms of an individual's contribution to corporate success. It was felt to be a myth that pay always accurately reflects an individual's performance.

Participants (all earning in excess of £100,000) were reluctant to describe themselves as 'highly paid'. They...could always point to people who earned more than them, who they considered highly paid

- Broadly, satisfaction with pay was wrapped up in the idea of entitlement, and the amount that participants' friends in similar companies earn is the arbiter of what they themselves feel entitled to.

Are we paying for risk?

- Participants who were members of senior management agreed that they took responsibility for risk, that the 'buck' stopped with them, and that they were ultimately responsible for the actions and behaviour of all their members of staff.
- But there was some debate about the exact nature of the risk; participants felt that earning more money would give you a cushion against losing your job, so the risk taken by junior members of staff would be higher in practice.

Is it about hard work?

- Interestingly, we did not hear participants cite their hard work as the primary rationale for high pay. Participants in our Opinions of High Earners survey in 2008, on the other hand, told us they felt they were on a treadmill of hard work which justified their high pay.
- Instead these participants said that market forces mean there is no alternative to high salaries in some industries.
- Therefore they do not feel they have to take personal responsibility for the system which pays them high salaries, or explain personally why they deserve salaries much higher than others.

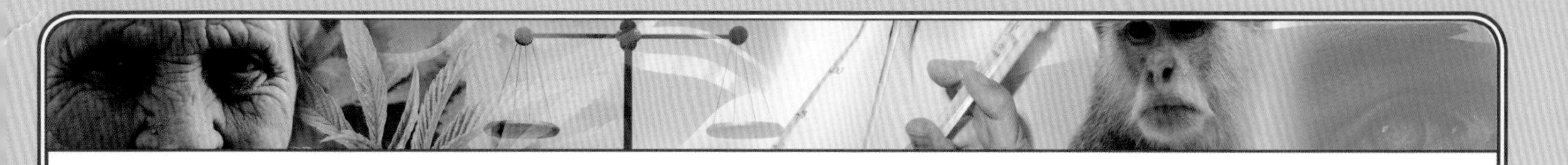

- Inequality is seen as systemic, rather than fair inequality on the basis of desert.

Do they know how they compare with the rest of society?

We discussed with participants where they felt they fitted on the income spectrum, and what words or phrases they used to describe their income.

- Participants (all earning in excess of £100,000) were reluctant to describe themselves as 'highly paid'. They knew they worked in industries which paid well, but could always point to people who earned more than them, who they considered highly paid.
- Because they experienced a need to work each day (in order to pay school fees or a mortgage), they did not feel 'rich'. We did not hear participants explicitly acknowledging the value of their assets in this equation (for example, I may be paying a high mortgage, and working hard, but I come out of this with a valuable house at the end of the day).
- The high earners we spoke to do not broach the subject of salaries with those in lower-paid industries. This creates an arguably slightly skewed view of entitlement, as they see their industry, and its pay thresholds, in a vacuum.

What about tax?

- Participants saw a justification for the 50% tax rate and accepted it; indeed, older participants, who had worked through the 1980s, felt that the current system of taxing high earners leaves them better off.
- However, there was a consensus that it should go no higher due to concerns about driving business away from the UK.
- Interestingly, there was a sense among some that, if this did happen, they might personally have to take steps to try and minimise the effect of tax on their own incomes.

But does it matter?

- While the participants recognised a public anger about high levels of pay, they saw some positive benefits of high earnings in society; they did not identify negative social or economic effects of high pay.
- The negative effects of income inequality were felt to be largely feelings of jealousy and hostility between those on different incomes.
- For some participants high salaries were perceived to trickle down into the wider economy.
- However, some questioned whether the highest salaries can be justified. The point at which salaries become 'too high to justify' tends to be at the point where an individual earns too much to realistically be able to spend.

Can the issue be addressed?

- The participants largely saw wage inequality as an institutional, global and systemic phenomenon and so changes would have to be on a global level.
- Those working in finance felt that the City could not be controlled from outside, by people who didn't understand it.
- Equally, participants also feel it cannot be controlled from within. Those working in finance in our study said that asking the City to behave differently is unlikely to work, as it only answers to its own rules.

July 2011

- The above information is the executive summary of *Just deserts, or good luck? High Earners' attitudes to pay*, a discussion paper produced by Ipsos MORI for the High Pay Commission, and is reprinted with permission. Visit http://highpaycommission.co.uk for more information.

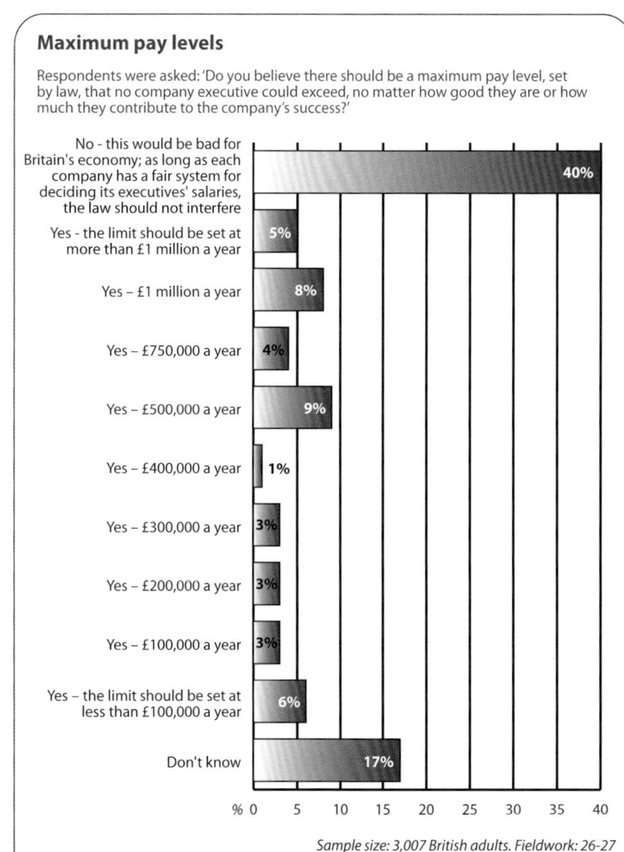

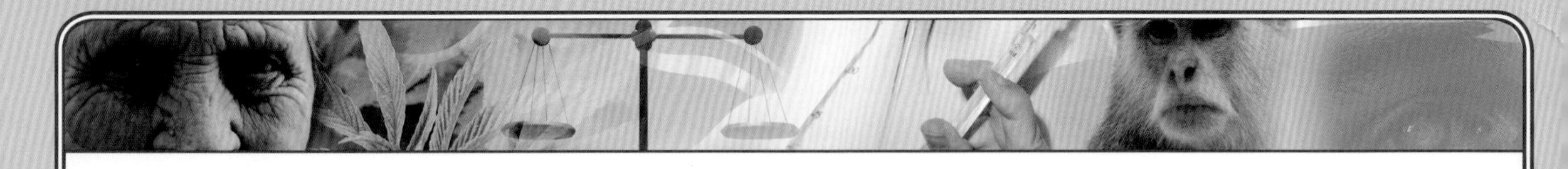

Cap bonuses, not benefits

Why are we so keen to punish the victims of the economic crisis instead of its perpetrators?

By Andrew Simms, NEF fellow

If nothing else, the habit of blaming the victims in times of economic crisis is remarkably consistent. Making the behaviour of people receiving welfare benefits in times of high structural unemployment the focus of debate, is a convenient political trick to distract attention from the failure of government economic policy. It was used repeatedly during recessions in the 1980s and 1990s by a government that thought high unemployment was 'a price worth paying' to control inflation.

If the discussion is about whether or not people are trying hard enough to find a job, it neatly suggests that the problem is with the individual rather than the state of the economy. As a divide-and-rule technique it is marvellously effective and immensely socially divisive. It pits the world (and especially the media) against the poor, and the poor against each other.

The Coalition's benefits bill may have been blocked by the House of Lords yesterday, but there remains a mainstream political consensus on the idea of introducing a cap on state support for people who are, or have been made, unemployed. Why is there no appetite for a cap on bonuses of those in the financial sector who caused the recession?

Average remuneration for the 1,200 most senior staff in financial services was £1.8 million in 2010, which means that pay for a single City worker in that group is equal to the total income of 69 families on capped benefits. Looked at more narrowly, the chief executive of nationalised bank RBS, Stephen Hester, is reportedly in line for a bonus that alone would be equal to the total income of 62 families surviving on capped benefits.

MPs are currently lobbying for a return to their own second home allowance scheme under which they could claim up to £25,000 (they can still claim a lot but it varies more now).

In terms of cause and effect, there's a degree to which the proposed cap on welfare benefits adds insult to injury. Because housing is a big part of the benefits bill, the suggestion is that if the families of the unemployed are living in accommodation, the cost of which would take them beyond the cap, then they should simply move to cheaper areas. But the housing market, especially in the South East, is heavily distorted by the fact that London is the centre of the astronomically high-paid financial services sector. If you're a top end City worker, a single bonus might buy you a home. As has been extensively reported, a big part of the reason that the crash happened was highly-rewarded private risk-taking in the housing market, that, because of the publicly guaranteed nature of banking, actually carried little risk for those banks that gambled and got it wrong.

So, not only have financial services triggered a recession leading to rising unemployment and families dependent on benefits, they've also driven up the cost of the housing in which the unemployed find themselves. If the poor are now forced to move to areas of the cheapest housing it will amount to a form of economic apartheid and ghettoisation. It's worth remembering, as the Bureau of Investigative Journalism revealed, that finance as a sector is by far the largest funder of the Conservative Party. Iain Duncan Smith effectively admitted on BBC Radio 4 that the Coalition Government that he was speaking on behalf of had not modelled the likely effects of the benefits cap proposal, but merely 'believed' it would not worsen homelessness. The danger is that the full social costs of the cap could, in a broader sense, cost far more than it is claimed it will save.

Now that even the International Monetary Fund (IMF) say that austerity measures have gone too far and are counterproductive to bringing about economic recovery, its easy to see the attractiveness of measures that create the impression of the problem lying elsewhere. Since the crisis began, we've witnessed the gymnastic ability with which the economic model's failure has been used by its advocates to push the very same model even further into our lives.

Instead of blaming the victims, the Government could stimulate the economy by investing in a brave new world of affordable social housing. It could prevent one mortgage-holding bank that has a public stake from repossessing the homes of victims of the recession. It could cap (if not abolish) bonuses in the City, or tax them at 100 per cent and invest the money in solving the housing crisis.

The trouble for the poor and unemployed compared to those employed in finance is not only their lack of power, but lack of voice. Every morning on television and radio business reports we still hear deferentially-treated the voices of those whose approach to the economy brought about the crisis. Perhaps the unemployed should be allowed a daily right of reply.

24 January 2012

⇨ The above information is reprinted with kind permission from the New Economics Foundation. Visit www.neweconomics.org for more information.

NEW ECONOMICS FOUNDATION

Business and human rights

A brief introduction.

Introduction

In the wake of major abuses in recent decades, civil society has increasingly called for companies to be held to human rights standards. Union Carbide was widely denounced for the 1984 Bhopal chemical gas leak that killed thousands in India. In the 1990s, non-governmental organisations (NGOs) campaigned against child labour and other abuses in the supply chains of prominent apparel and footwear companies. They also denounced alleged abuses by mining, oil and gas companies, including complicity in violence by government security forces and pollution that damaged the health of people in nearby communities.

In the past companies tended to approach social issues through their corporate social responsibility (CSR) programmes. However, many CSR initiatives were undertaken selectively, based on what the company voluntarily chose to address. A human rights approach requires companies to respect all human rights; they do not have the option of picking and choosing to deal with only those issues with which they feel comfortable. A human rights framework provides a universally recognised, people-centred approach to companies' social & environmental impacts.

In the wake of major abuses in recent decades, civil society has increasingly called for companies to be held to human rights standards

The United Nations launched the voluntary Global Compact in 2000, and appointed a Special Representative on business & human rights in 2005. The UN Human Rights Council endorsed the 'Guiding Principles on Business and Human Rights' drafted by the Special Representative in June 2011. The Guiding Principles were designed to implement the 'Protect, Respect and Remedy' policy framework that the Special Representative had proposed and the Council had approved in 2008. This framework consists of the state duty to protect against human rights abuses; the corporate responsibility to respect human rights; and greater access by victims to effective remedies. Also in 2011, the Council established a Working Group on business & human rights, and an annual Forum on business & human rights, to be organised by the Working Group.

Companies have joined together, in some cases with governments, international organizations and/or NGOs, in voluntary initiatives to address some human rights issues. An increasing number of companies are taking positive steps to promote human rights. But the daily reports on our site of abuses by companies demonstrate that much remains to be done.

The context

Every company in every industry sector has human rights impacts and responsibilities. As demonstrated on our website, companies can impact the entire range of human rights issues positively or negatively, including discrimination, sexual harassment, health & safety, freedom of association and to form unions, rape, torture, freedom of expression, privacy, poverty, food and water, education and housing.

Companies have long been accused of responsibility for human rights abuses. Some examples:

- Historical abuses: Companies profited from slavery and the slave trade; providing goods and services to Nazi Germany that enabled war crimes and crimes against humanity; forced labour in Asia during World War II; selling to the apartheid government in South Africa and military governments in Latin America products that they used in perpetrating abuses.
- Killings: Blackwater (now Academi) was sued over shootings in Baghdad in 2007 that left 17 civilians dead.
- Environmental health: A US-owned company operated an outdated lead smelter in La Oroya, Peru – 99% of children in the area were found to have unacceptably high levels of lead in their blood.
- Rape & sexual abuse: Multinational beer companies hire 'beer promotion women' in Cambodia to promote their products in bars. But many companies allegedly do not do enough to protect the women (who are often teenagers) from rape and abuse.
- Torture: Security companies hired by international diamond firms in Cuango, Angola, were reportedly responsible for beatings, attacks with machetes, sexual abuse, torture and killings. The victims were artisanal miners.
- Child labour: Uzbekistan forces children to work in cotton fields without pay, then sells the cotton on to international markets, where it is bought and used by major companies.
- Freedom of expression: Yahoo! China handed over private user data about dissidents to the Chinese Government; the government imprisoned the dissidents.

BUSINESS AND HUMAN RIGHTS RESOURCE CENTRE

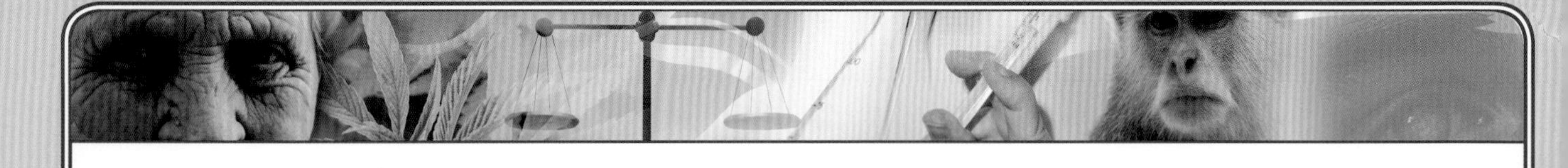

- Indigenous peoples & displacement: In India, a mining company is accused of displacing a tribal group from its traditional lands without obtaining consent or providing adequate compensation.
- Complicity: Burmese soldiers providing security for a pipeline that was developed by major oil companies forced villagers to work on the pipeline and shot and tortured protesters.
- Discrimination: Wal-Mart has been accused in a lawsuit of systematically discriminating against over 90,000 of its female employees in USA. Some employers in France have insisted that employment agencies refer only white workers to them, according to prosecutors.

Some historically maintained that human rights standards were only applicable to governments, not the private sector

- Labour rights: Foreign companies operating in Colombia have been sued for allegedly paying paramilitaries who intimidated and killed union leaders.
- Access to water: In India, beverage companies have allegedly depleted groundwater supplies in rural villages.
- Workplace safety: Hundreds die every year in Chinese coal mines.

Companies have a responsibility to respect human rights

Some historically maintained that human rights standards were only applicable to governments, not the private sector. Some companies claimed that their sole obligation was to respect national laws, even where those laws failed to meet international human rights standards.

However, the preamble to the Universal Declaration calls on 'every individual and every organ of society' to promote and respect human rights. Leading international law scholar Louis Henkin noted in 1999 that 'every individual and every organ of society excludes no one, no company, no market, no cyberspace. The Universal Declaration applies to them all.' A 2002 report by the International Council on Human Rights Policy, Beyond Voluntarism: Human rights and the developing international legal obligations of companies, states that 'there is a clear basis in international law for extending international legal obligations to companies in relation to human rights.'

Although the primary duty to protect human rights remains with national governments, companies have a responsibility to respect human rights in their operations. The UN Human Rights Council endorsed the Guiding Principles on Business and Human Rights by consensus in 2011. Guiding Principle 11 states: 'Business enterprises should respect human rights. This means that they should avoid infringing on the human rights of others and should address adverse human rights impacts with which they are involved.' The official commentaries to the Guiding Principles on Business and Human Rights, endorsed by the UN Human Rights Council, state: 'The responsibility to respect human rights is a global standard of expected conduct for all business enterprises wherever they operate...[It] exists over and above compliance with national laws and regulations protecting human rights.'

- The above information is an extract from the Business and Human Rights Resource Centre's briefing *Business and human rights – a brief introduction* and is reprinted with permission. Visit www.business-humanrights.org for more information.

Respondents were asked: 'Thinking generally about senior executives in big British companies, do you agree or disagree with the following statements?'

It is vital for some major British companies to pay their senior executives more than £1 million a year, in order to attract the best talent and ensure that their companies do well.

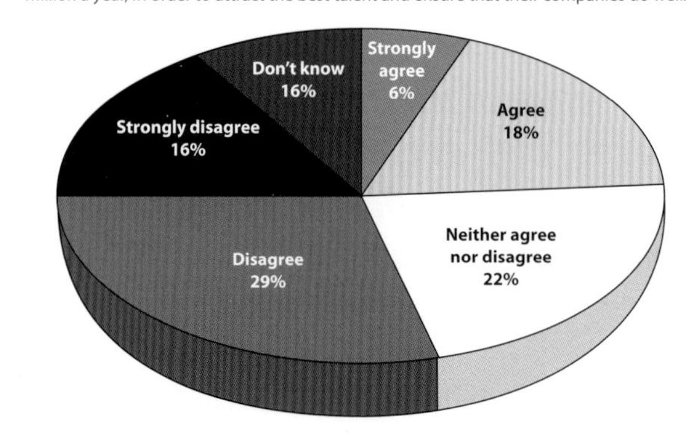

Senior executives in big British companies generally do not work as hard as the other people in their companies.

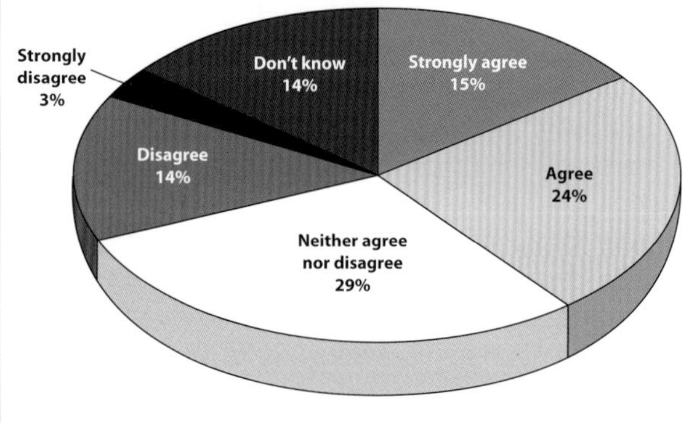

Sample size: 3,007 British adults. Fieldwork: 26-27 June 2011. Source: YouGov (www.yougov.com)

BUSINESS AND HUMAN RIGHTS RESOURCE CENTRE

Forced labour

What is the dilemma?

'How can a company practically and responsibly identify and address problems of forced labour in lower tiers of its supply chain, particularly when it extends into areas or sectors known to use forced labour?'

The dilemma for business is how to address the presence of forced labour within its supply chain responsibly, as it can be difficult to define as well as detect. Forced labour often does not occur within a company's operations as stringent procedures will be in place to ensure good working practices. However, forced labour can be found further down the supply chain, especially when multi-national companies (MNCs) source from countries where there is a high amount of poverty and a lack of legal protection and/or where it is common practice to use recruitment agencies and labour providers, where there is no legal requirement for such businesses to be registered or meet certain standards.

A factor that makes forced labour difficult to detect relates to the presence of migrant workers, particularly those with no or false documentation, as they are vulnerable and reluctant to admit to or report their forced labour status. More challenging circumstances arise where labour is trafficked and transported from their home countries, especially where families rely on victims for financial support.

According to Anti-Slavery International, discrimination is one of the root causes of slavery in the 21st century. However, it is also the vulnerable and poorest members of the community, including immigrants, minorities, children and women, who are victims of forced labour. People in these groups are often easily exploited as it can be difficult for them to find employment opportunities and they are often forced to work in sub-standard working environments.

Furthermore, forced labour can take different forms: workers may still be paid but are bonded to debts that they cannot work their way out of; some are trafficked for both sexual exploitation and forced labour abroad without means to return to their home state and some are forced by the state to undertake labour vital to the country's economy.

Real-world examples

Toyota, GM and Kohler accused of purchasing goods made from pig iron produced by forced labourers

A 2 November 2006 Bloomberg article, *Slaves in Amazon Forced to Make Material Used in Cars*,[1] reported that workers found in government raids in the Tucurui area of the Brazilian Amazon had not collected wages in several months and could not afford to leave. It is reported that some workers were 800km from home, working in extreme heat without access to medical facilities or clean water. These workers were burning hardwood to produce charcoal. This charcoal is used in the production of pig iron, which is then used in the production of steel for use in the manufacturing of a wide range of goods made by MNCs, including auto parts, tractors, sinks and appliances.

MNCs including General Motors, Kohler, Toyota and Whirlpool have all reportedly purchased steel made from pig iron produced by forced labour, for the manufacturing of their products. Steel made from pig iron that is produced by forced labour is currently hard to trace as it is often sourced from a third party.

The dilemma for a company is how to procure steel in an ethically responsible manner when it operates in countries where the use of forced labour is significant.

HUMAN RIGHTS AND BUSINESS DILEMMAS FORUM

H&M and Zara purchased garments made from Uzbek cotton picked by forced child labourers

An Anti-Slavery International campaign has accused large retailing companies, including Tesco, Wal-Mart/ Asda, H&M and Zara, of being complicit in purchasing products made from Uzbek cotton which is picked by forced child labourers. An estimated two million children between the ages of 11 and 17 harvest cotton in Uzbekistan under conditions described as forced labour.[2] Unlike cases where children work on family farms, the Uzbek case is different in scale, organisation and government complicity. Each year, for example, the Government closes schools, hospitals and offices for three months in order to boost the workforce available for the annual cotton harvest, with student, teachers and government employees participating in the process.

The Responsible Cotton Network says some school administrators have used physical abuse and public humiliation to ensure that the Government-imposed quota of 30–60 kilograms of cotton is picked per child per day, depending on their age.[3] Children receive little or no pay for their work, and are often only provided with food. Uzbekistan is the world's third largest cotton exporter and earns approximately US$1 billion annually.[4]

As yet, there is no international mechanism to properly trace the source of cotton, although such a process is in the development stages. This makes it a complicated undertaking for any company that has a policy stating that it will not knowingly source cotton to practically address this policy.

Major Western companies accused of purchasing Malaysian hard disk drives made by forced labourers

On 21 April 2008, a *Newsweek* article entitled 'Lured into Bondage'[5] reported that foreign workers at a Malaysian company, Local Technic Industry, were subject to bonded labour conditions. This company makes cast-aluminium bodies for the hard disk drives, which are purchased by Western companies (including Western Digital) who distribute them onto the US market. It is reported that many major computer companies purchase these hard disk drives.

According to the report, migrant workers were lured into working in Malaysia. Upon arrival these workers (by law) are forced to sign multiple-year contracts and surrender their passports to their employers. If these migrant workers try to leave work during their employment they may be arrested and imprisoned by the authorities. These workers' living expenses are deducted from their wage, leaving very little at the end of the pay period. One worker, for example, made US$14 a month after all living expenses and taxes were deducted. This amounted to an annual salary of US$504.

The dilemma for an electronic company is how it can trace the use of its many electronic components to ensure that it does not source from companies that are likely to hire forced labour.

Notes

1. Bloomberg, *Slaves in Amazon Forced to Make Material Used in Cars*, http://www.bloomberg.com/apps/news?pid=20601082&sid=a4j1VKZq34TM
2. *Los Angeles Times*, 'Hard truths about Uzbek cotton', http://www.latimes.com/news/opinion/commentary/la-oe-harkin25-2009sep25,0,3490812.story
3. As you Sow, *Update on forced and child labour in Uzbekistan*, http://www.asyousow.org/human_rights/labor_uzbek.shtml
4. Environmental Justice Foundation, *Slave Nation – State-sponsored forced child labour in Uzbekistan's cotton fields*, http://www.ejfoundation.org/pdf/slave_nation.pdf
5. *Newsweek*, 21 April 2008, 'Lured ILO, Forced Labour: Coercion and exploitation in the private economy', http://www.ilo.org/wcmsp5/groups/public/---ed_norm/---declaration/documents/publication/wcms_112966.pdf

⇨ The above information is reprinted with kind permission from the Human Rights and Business Dilemmas Forum. Visit http://human-rights.unglobalcompact.org for more.

Does business behave ethically?

Respondents were asked: 'There is a lot of discussion these days about how ethically business is behaving – that is, how far its behaviour and decisions follow good principles. How ethically do you think British business generally behaves?'

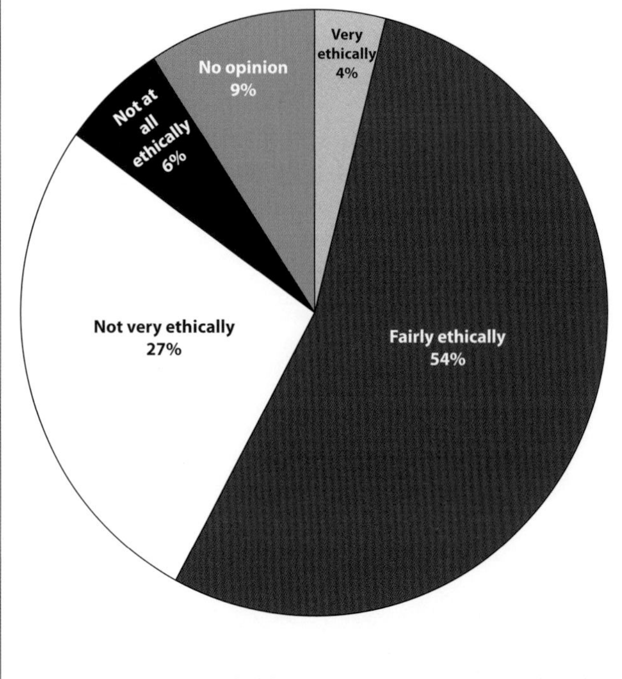

Base: 1,001 British adults aged 16+. Fieldwork: 19-25 August 2011, face to face methodology. Source: Corporate Responsibility Attitudes of the British public – Ethics in Business *(report for Institute of Business Ethics). Ipsos MORI.*

Why eliminating corruption is crucial to sustainability

Bribery and corruption present significant risks to business and tackling them increases an organisation's resilience to shocks.

Ethical business practices are a critical aspect of sustainability, yet progress towards eliminating bribery and corruption appears to be elusive in the face of persistent headlines such as the recent forced resignation of Avon CEO Andrea Jung, the IKEA incident in Russia and the conviction of former French President Jacques Chirac.

Corruption continues to have a dire effect on the global economy. In fact, the World Bank and the World Economic Forum estimate that corruption costs more than 5% of global GDP ($2.6 trillion) annually, and estimate that more than $1 trillion is paid in bribes annually. These organisations suggest that corruption adds 10% to the total cost of doing business globally, and a staggering 25% to the cost of procurement contracts in developing countries.

Why should companies care? Firstly, corruption is illegal. Secondly, it distorts competition and free markets. And third: it incentivises and rewards unethical behaviour. The bottom line is that corruption hinders social and economic growth, delays the emergence of developing economies and stunts thriving democracies based on good governance and the rule of law.

Unlike other white-collar crimes such as fraud, serious international efforts to combat corruption are almost nascent by comparison. Today, there is a UN Convention Against Corruption, the OECD Bribery Convention, and businesses may also participate in voluntary initiatives, such as the UN Global Compact and the Extractive Industries Transparency Initiative.

National legislation such as the 1998 US Foreign Corrupt Practices Act (FCPA) and the 2010 UK Bribery Act seek to punish corruption regardless of where it occurs in the world. FCPA enforcement is a high priority for the Securities and Exchange Commission (SEC), with 12 cases prosecuted in 2011 and 16 cases in 2010. Companies including Alcoa, Daimler AG and Siemens AG have been charged under FCPA with Siemens, for one, obliged to pay a record $1.6 billion in fines. The new UK law is expected to provoke similar prosecutions, high-profile convictions, costly fines and lawsuits.

It is not enough, however, to view bribery and corruption as a simple regulatory or compliance issue. A corporate culture that appears to tolerate or even reward maverick behaviour or rule-breaking is vulnerable to corruption. Accusations of bribery or corruption can destroy a company's good reputation and take years to repair, while fines and lawsuits can severely damage a company's social licence to operate.

On the other hand, an effective 'no bribes' policy and a culture where strong business values and ethical behaviour are central facets, potentially offers the competitive advantages of transparency: a cleaner corporate image, more trustworthy business relationships, lower costs and less litigious shareholders.

The World Bank and the World Economic Forum estimate that corruption costs more than 5% of global GDP ($2.6 trillion) annually, and estimate that more than $1 trillion is paid in bribes annually

Unfortunately, having a corporate code of conduct or ethics is not a panacea – especially in the absence of globally accepted ethical norms. Corporate policies must be values-based but driven by strong leadership, clear governance structures, best practice benchmarking, specialised due diligence, training, monitoring and review mechanisms, and effective channels for whistleblowers.

Corruption, in all its forms, is always a business risk. Some operating environments clearly pose higher risks than others, such as jurisdictions with weak governance or lack of rule of law, resource-rich or in rapid growth economies, or where transactions involve middlemen or state monopolies.

Addressing the challenges of combating bribery and corruption need not be overwhelming. In fact, it offers a major opportunity for companies to boost their own sustainability and resilience to shocks.

Doug Bannerman is Vice-President, Two Tomorrows (North America) and David Roberts is Associate, Two Tomorrows (Europe).

17 January 2012

THE GUARDIAN

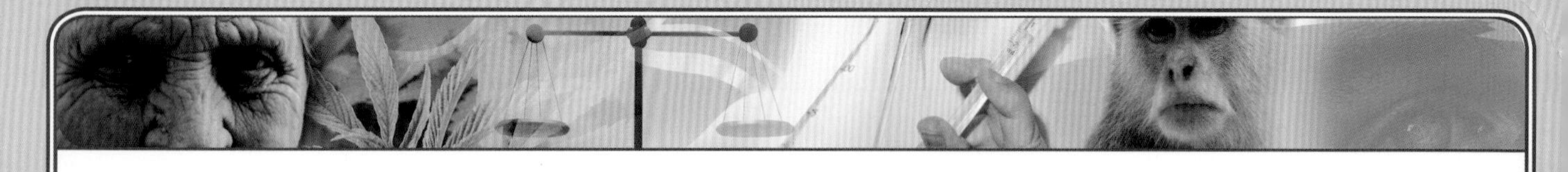

Tax and corporate responsibility

Information from Tax Research UK.

Introduction

Tax paid is, arguably, the strongest indicator of a corporation's social responsibility that there is.

I hope no major corporation evades tax. Tax evasion is illegal. I think that without exception major corporations avoid tax.

What tax avoidance is

Tax avoidance is legal. Tax avoidance exploits the loopholes in tax law to ensure that less tax is paid than those creating that legislation expected. This can be done in individual states, where, however, it is relatively easy for governments to combat it. For multinational corporations there is a much more lucrative opportunity for tax avoidance. That comes from exploiting the loopholes that exist between the laws of different states.

The opportunity for international tax avoidance is based on three variables. The first is the number of companies making up a multinational corporation: the more companies there are in a group the easier it is to avoid tax.

Second is the willingness of the multinational corporation to use tax haven corporations to hide the true substance of transactions they undertake from view. Tax haven entities never file accounts on public record, and if used solely for intra-group transactions by a multinational corporation are also totally lost from view in the group accounts sent to shareholders. But they can move profit, and so tax savings, almost endlessly around the world.

Thirdly, the greater the opportunity a multinational corporation has to create intangible assets the easier it is to shift profits to avoid tax.

Tax avoidance exploits the loopholes in tax law to ensure that less tax is paid than those creating that legislation expected

All of this activity is, apparently, acceptable behaviour. Indeed, creating mechanisms to assist corporations avoid tax is seen as an honourable professional activity to be well rewarded, with its practitioners treated as being worthy of esteem.

Tax avoidance is avoiding your obligations

This is bizarre when viewed from the perspective of society as a whole. The clue to that fact is within the name of the activity. To avoid paying tax means you are avoiding your obligation to a government that represents a society. No other interpretation of the activity is possible. Society expects tax to be paid. Tax avoiders work out ways to not pay. In the process they inevitably value their interests as more important than those of society. As a result it is just not possible to avoid tax and be corporately socially responsible.

Tax compliance

To be responsible a corporation has to be tax compliant. Tax compliance is seeking to pay the right amount of tax (but no more) in the right place at the right time where right means that the economic substance of the transactions undertaken coincides with the place and form in which they are reported for taxation purposes.

Tax compliance does not bring an end to tax planning. Far from it: the ambiguities in tax law will remain forever; the uncertainties inherent in the interpretation of language guarantee that. But tax-compliant behaviour is based on a completely different mindset to tax avoidance.

Tax compliance says that paying tax is the duty a corporation has to all the societies in which it operates, without exception. In addition it says that the payment made should reflect the real value the corporation has

TAX RESEARCH UK

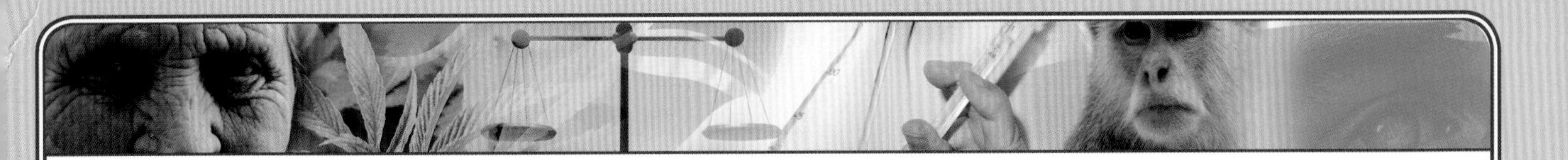

generated in the jurisdiction to which the tax is due. This contrasts with tax avoidance where the amount paid will be the minimum amount it can get away with in any place.

Evidencing tax and corporate responsibility

But like all responsible actions, payment of tax must be evidenced. This is also possible. A method of accounting called country-by-country reporting requires multinational corporations to publish profit and loss accounts and limited balance sheet data for every country in which they operate, without exception. That would, of course, reveal tax paid by country. This is essential because it shows what is, in effect, the payment a multinational corporation has made to a state for the right to operate within that jurisdiction.

That right to operate is granted using exactly the same process used to create tax law. Statute law creates the limited liability corporation, with all the privileges that go with it. Statute law creates the obligation to pay tax, with all the responsibilities that go with it. These are two sides of the same coin. The licence to operate inherent in the act of incorporation under law carries with it the obligation to pay the taxes properly demanded by the state that granted that right to operate on behalf of the people of the jurisdiction in question.

That's why tax is the strongest indicator of a corporation's social responsibility that there is. And that's why multinational corporations should report their compliance with the obligation to pay, country by country, without exception, to ensure they are accountable to those people throughout the world who grant them their right to operate.

May 2010

⇨ The above information is reprinted with kind permission from Tax Research UK. Visit www.taxresearch.org.uk for more information.

Investors should make tax an ethical issue

Investors who want to ensure their money supports ethical concerns should add tax behaviour to the criteria by which companies are judged, Christian Aid says today.

'Along with traditional concerns such as involvement in tobacco, weapons and environmental issues, a company should also be assessed on its tax practices,' says Dr David McNair, Christian Aid's Principal Adviser on Economic Justice.

'Companies should contribute to the societies in which they work. Paying tax is a major way in which they can do so, helping fund schools, hospitals and other essential public services.

'To qualify as an ethical investment, Christian Aid believes a company must pay its taxes in a transparent way. This includes paying the taxes they owe in the countries where the work which generated the profits actually took place.

'Some unscrupulous multinational corporations use the secrecy offered by the world's tax havens to avoid, or even evade, the tax they owe, which has a particularly damaging impact on the poorer countries where they operate.

'At present, we estimate that tax dodging by multinationals costs developing countries some $160 billion a year in lost tax revenue – one-and-a-half times the amount they receive from rich countries in aid. This harms millions of people living in poverty.'

In a report published this week calling for tax to be regarded as a corporate responsibility issue, Christian Aid warns that companies which pursue aggressive tax strategies face a higher risk of reputational damage than those that don't. They also risk costly legal action being taken against them by tax authorities.

The report argues that companies should consider implementing codes of conduct which rule out aggressive tax behaviour and include commitments such as:

- income is held to be taxable in the country where it was generated;
- tax planning will seek to comply with the spirit as well as the letter of the law;
- tax planning will be consistently disclosed to all tax authorities it affects;
- information about transactions will be consistently disclosed to all the tax authorities involved.

7 October 2011

⇨ The above information is reprinted with kind permission from Christian Aid. Visit www.christianaid.org.uk for more information.

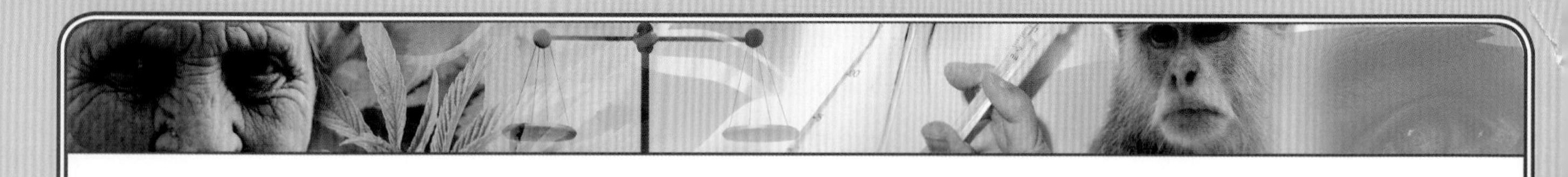

Huge cost of tax evasion revealed as campaign to tackle tax havens launches

Information from Tax Justice Network.

New research published by the Tax Justice Network shows that tax evasion costs 145 countries, representing over 98% of world GDP, more than US$3.1 trillion annually.

In the UK for instance, a staggering £69.9 billion a year is lost to tax evasion in the 'shadow economy' – that is, 56% of the country's total healthcare spend.

Tax havens are a major part of the tax evasion problem – and these new findings come as the Tax Justice Network launches Tackle Tax Havens, a new campaign aimed at the general public that highlights the critical role that these secretive states play in corrupting the global economy.

The issue of tax collection is rising fast up the political and social agenda, as countries across the world make deep cuts in public spending and increase taxes in ways that hurt the poor and the middle classes the most.

This new research demonstrates how important it is to tackle tax evasion and the tax havens that help wealthy individuals and organisations escape from contributing to the services that directly benefit them – from the health and education systems that support their workforces, to the roads that ship their goods to markets, to the courts of law that enforce their contracts or to the police who protect their property.

But tax havens are not just about tax: they cause colossal damage on many fronts. Tackle Tax Havens aims to arm the general public with a solid working knowledge of the offshore system and the problems it causes – and to show what we can do about it.

Other key findings of the new report include:

- Europe as a whole loses the equivalent of 87% of its total healthcare budget to tax evasion, while Africa loses 98% and South America 139%.
- Over the 145 countries surveyed, an unweighted average of 110% of the annual healthcare budget was lost to tax evasion.
- 119 of the 145 countries surveyed are losing over half of their healthcare budget to tax evasion.
- In 67 countries, tax evasion losses are larger than their entire health budgets.
- In Bolivia, tax evasion is more than four times as large as that oil-rich country's health spending. In Russia, it is more than three times the size.
- More than $1 in every $6 earned in the world is not subject to tax because those earning it have deliberately ensured that their income is hidden from the world's tax authorities.
- In Greece and Italy, where economic collapse currently looks possible, more than €1 in €4 is hidden in the shadow economy.

John Christensen, Director of the Tax Justice Network, said: 'Tackling tax havens is a crucial part of ending the culture of tax evasion. Tax evasion is crippling public finances across the world but governments aren't doing nearly enough to end this cancer.

'Tax havens are engaged in economic warfare against the tax regimes of sovereign countries, and these estimates reveal the human cost in terms of the impact on health services.'

Richard Murphy of Tax Research UK, who undertook the research for the Tax Justice Network, said: 'New data from the World Bank published last year on the size of countries' shadow economies let us prepare this estimate of tax lost to criminal tax evasion annually. The findings add a new policy agenda to public debate on the world's financial crisis. For example, Italy loses €183 billion to tax evasion a year. Its current debt of €1.9 trillion represents just over ten years' tax of tax evasion on this basis. If only more had been done to tackle rampant tax evasion, Europe would not be facing a crisis today.

'Tax havens can be beaten using three simple measures. First we demand that all tax havens put details of the ownership of all companies and trusts located there, and the accounts of those organisations, on public record. Second we demand that all multinational companies publish accounts that reveal their use of tax havens. Last, we believe that all tax havens should be required to exchange information each year on the income recorded within them belonging to the citizens of other countries with the places where those people really live.

'These measures would shatter the secrecy of tax havens for good, and that means those committing tax crimes will no longer have places to hide the proceeds of their crimes. Nothing could make a bigger contribution than this to solving the world's financial crisis right now.'

25 November 2011

➪ The above information is reprinted with kind permission from the Tax Justice Network. Visit www.taxjustice.net for more information.

TAX JUSTICE NETWORK

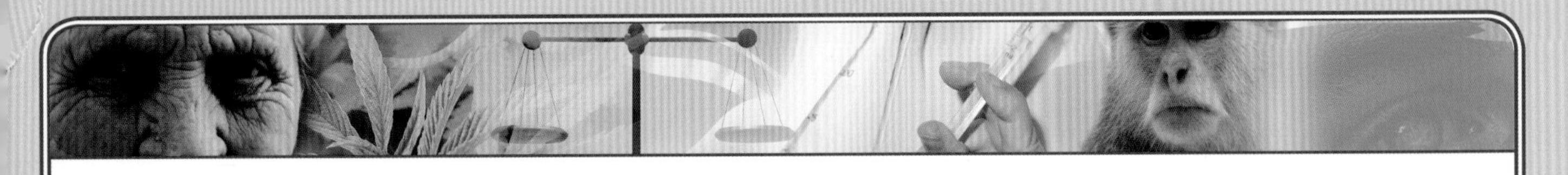

Addicted to tax havens

The secret life of the FTSE 100.

The full extent to which FTSE 100 companies use tax havens has, for the first time, been compiled, analysed and published in an accessible and searchable format by ActionAid.

Of the 100 biggest groups listed on the London Stock Exchange, 98 use tax havens. ActionAid's research shows just how embedded the use of tax havens is in the structures of nearly all Britain's biggest companies.

The findings are of particular concern because many FTSE 100 groups are set to benefit from plans currently under consideration by the Treasury to give multinational companies using tax havens an £840 million tax break, by relaxing the very rules designed to prevent tax-haven abuse.

An expanded tax revenue base in developing countries is the only sustainable source of funding for governments to invest in reducing poverty and inequality. It means that they don't need to depend on aid and can achieve self-reliance. Yet the OECD estimates that developing countries lose almost three times more to tax havens than all the aid they receive each year. Spent effectively, this sum would easily be sufficient to achieve the Millennium Development Goals.

Tax haven effective corporate rates

Jurisdiction	Effective corporate tax rate
Jersey	0%
Cayman Islands	0%
Mauritius	3%
Ireland	12.5%
Hong Kong	16.5%

Corporate tax avoidance, one of the main reasons companies use tax havens, has a massive impact on developing and developed countries alike. The lack of transparency makes it difficult for developing country tax authorities to identify and collect taxes owed by global companies operating in their countries.

With this in mind, ActionAid's research raises serious questions about many of Britain's best known businesses. How has the use of tax havens reached such epidemic levels? What is the impact on the UK exchequer, the stability of the international financial system and the ability of developing countries to raise tax revenues to invest in reducing poverty?

ActionAid found that:

- The FTSE 100 largest groups registered on the London Stock Exchange comprise 34,216 subsidiary companies, joint ventures and associates.
- 38% (8,492) of their overseas companies are located in tax havens.
- 98 groups declared tax haven companies, with only two groups, Fresnillo and Hargreaves Landsdown, who did not.
- The banking sector makes heaviest use of tax havens, with a total of 1,649 tax haven companies between the 'big four' banks. They are by far the biggest users of the Cayman Islands, where Barclays alone has 174 companies.
- The biggest tax haven user overall is the advertising company WPP, which has 611 tax haven companies.
- The FTSE 100 companies make much more use of tax havens than their American equivalents.
- There are over 600 FTSE 100 subsidiary companies in Jersey (more than in the whole of China), 400 in the Cayman Islands and 300 in Luxembourg – all tiny tax havens.

We believe that the FTSE 100 have big questions to answer about why they require such a massive number of companies registered in tax havens. While this piece of research in itself does not prove tax avoidance, it highlights the extent of these multinational groups' operations in places that provide tax advantages and help obscure information.

In recent times, politicians around the world and across the political spectrum have talked tough on cracking down on the use of tax havens to avoid taxes. With both developing and developed countries continuing to suffer the effects of the global financial crisis, decisive action to tackle tax havens from both the UK Government and G20 leaders is well overdue.

ACTIONAID

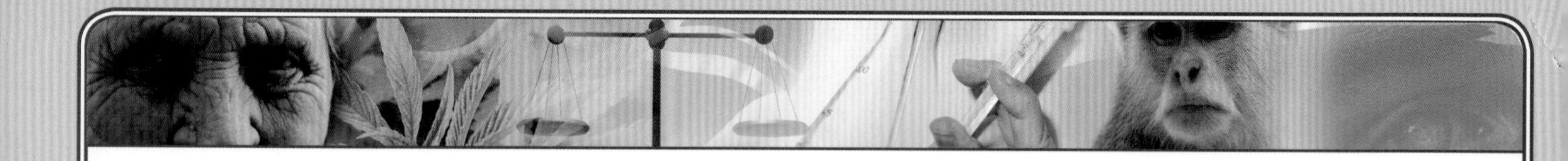

The banks and the financial sector are by far the heaviest users of tax havens

'Much of the shadow banking sector, a major contributor to the economic crisis, was also only possible because of tax haven secrecy.' *Vince Cable MP, 2009*

The global financial crisis has caused hardship around the world and was originally triggered by the reckless over-reaching of the banks and financial sector. The first meeting of G20 leaders in London in April 2009 identified that the catalyst of the crisis was a toxic mix of complex financial products routed through tax havens.

Our research shows that despite efforts to clean up the banking sector, banks are still doing a brisk business via tax havens. The big four high street banks have 1,649 tax haven subsidiaries between them – more than half of all their 3,067 overseas subsidiaries.

Jersey: top ten users

Company	Number
The British Land Company	143
Lloyds Banking Group	72
Barclays	35
HSBC	31
The Royal Bank of Scotland Group	25
The Capita Group	19
Randgold Resources	19
British American Tobacco	18
Schroders	18
Petrofac Inc.	16

Luxembourg: top ten users

Company	Number
WPP	33
Anglo American	30
Prudential	22
Lloyds Banking Group	18
The Royal Bank of Scotland Group	17
The British Land Company	16
HSBC	14
Barclays	13
Reckitt Benckiser	12
Vodafone Group	11

Cayman Islands: top 10 users

Company	Number
Barclays	174
The Royal Bank of Scotland Group	37
HSBC	30
Lloyds Banking Group	26
International Power	20
Standard Chartered	17
Prudential	15
Tesco	14
BP	10
Man Group	10

HSBC is the biggest financial sector user of tax havens in the FTSE 100, with a grand total of 556. Some other figures are particularly revealing:

- Barclays has 174 companies located in the Cayman Islands alone.
- Lloyds group has 97 companies in the Channel Islands.
- HSBC has 156 companies in the US state of Delaware, compared to 97 in the rest of the USA.

Although the banks are largely profitable again, they are still getting a fantastic deal on their tax bills. This is partly because of their tax avoidance, and partly because they are carrying forward losses made during the financial crisis. In the last budget, the Government gave banking and finance companies a tax break worth £80 million per year when it changed the way their foreign branches were taxed.

The offshore invasion

It's not only the banks who are making such big use of tax havens. Our research reveals startling facts about many other companies:

- Oil and mining companies comprise the other big group of tax haven users. BP and Shell have almost 1,000 tax haven companies between them, including more than 100 in the Caribbean (hardly a major source of oil). The extractive industries often operate in developing countries, where natural resources play a central economic role.
- British American Tobacco has a massive 200 companies in tax havens. It is also one of the most prevalent in developing countries.
- There are also some surprises: all our supermarkets use tax haven structures – perhaps expected in the case of global behemoth Tesco, but not so for UK-only retailers such as Morrisons and Sainsbury's.

Many of these companies are 'mailbox' companies, which are often used as part of tax avoidance schemes. They exist in name only and are usually administered by offshore law firms. In locations such as Mauritius, Jersey and Delaware we have identified hundreds of subsidiaries owned by dozens of different multinationals that are registered at a handful of individual addresses, belonging to offshore law firms.

October 2011

- The above information is an extract from the ActionAid report *Addicted to tax havens: The secret life of the FTSE 100* and is reprinted with permission. Visit www.actionaid.org.uk to view the full text. You can view an interactive map showing information from the report here: www.actionaid.org.uk/taxhavens

ACTIONAID

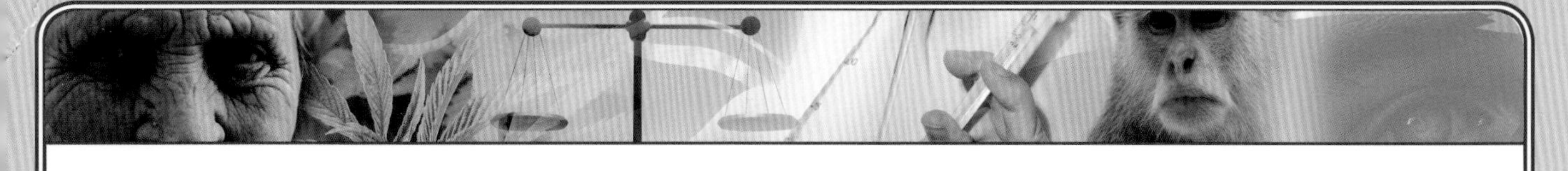

The ethical challenges of social media

This briefing aims to raise awareness of the ethical challenges social media presents for companies and considers good practice in providing guidance for employees on its use, whether for business or personal use.

Social media and business ethics

Social media is an umbrella term used to describe social interaction through a suite of technology-based tools, many of which are Internet-based. This includes, but is not limited to, Internet forums, networking sites such as Facebook, Twitter, LinkedIn and Google Plus, webcasts and blogs.

Social media exhibits unique characteristics when compared to 'traditional' media forms. Its speed and scope means that once content is published it is available instantaneously, to a potentially global audience. Social media tools tend to be free or available at a very low cost relative to other forms of media and do not require users to have much technical knowledge. This allows larger numbers of individuals to access and publish material than with traditional media forms.

my blog entry: some **private** thoughts

not anymore!

Social media is usually interactive in a way that traditional media is not, so users can comment on and edit published material, making it difficult to control content. Social media blurs private/public boundaries when individuals' personal information and opinions enter the public domain. The boundaries between personal and work life also become blurred as companies make use of social media (originally designed for personal use) for business purposes, and likewise employees access personal sites while at work. A 2011 DLA Piper survey found social media is used for personal and work-related activities by 95% of employees.

These unique characteristics of social media pose ethical challenges for business, through employees' use of social media on behalf of the company, as well as their personal use. The news headlines in Box 1 provide examples of these challenges.

Box 1: Headlines relating to social media in 2011

'Bayer rapped for tweeting about medicines'

'Cyber bullying more harmful'

'Online monitoring of job candidates raises disturbing questions'

'Third of firms forced to discipline workers over social media tweets and updates'

The ethical challenges

'While the decision to post videos, pictures, thoughts, experiences and observations to social networking sites is personal, a single act can create far-reaching ethical consequences for individuals as well as organisations.' *Sharon Allen, chairman of the board, Deloitte LLP*

Integrity risk

In an IBE survey of large companies, six of seven respondents identified integrity risk as the main ethical challenge with regard to social media. When an employee uses social media in an irresponsible way either on behalf of the company or through their personal social media account, it can undermine the company's commitment to ethical practice and expose it to integrity risk.

The case of Nestlé provides an example. In March 2011, an employee who was managing content on the company's Facebook 'Fan Page' posted offensive

INSTITUTE OF BUSINESS ETHICS

comments in response to negative remarks by 'fans'. The employee's behaviour violated the company's business principle of integrity and their commitment to 'avoid any conduct that could damage or risk Nestlé or its reputation' and provoked a consumer backlash. Amidst calls to boycott Nestlé, members of the general public also joined the Fan Page specifically to criticise the company.

Alternatively, employees might post negative comments about the company on their personal social media profile. This is harder for companies to control. The DLA Piper survey found that one-third of employers had disciplined staff for inappropriate comments about the company on social media sites.

To ensure that work-related discussion amongst employees is internal to the organisation, Serco Group, a large UK-listed international services company, has developed an 'internal Facebook'. This is for staff to use to discuss work topics with colleagues rather than using public forums, as a way of dealing with integrity risk.

The scope and speed of social media make it an effective medium through which companies market themselves and their products/services. With any form of marketing, companies have a duty to market responsibly. The interactive nature of social media provides companies with the ability to engage with customers more directly than other forms of media. This poses new ethical challenges.

It has become common practice for companies to create profiles on social networking sites to advertise their goods and services. To avoid misleading consumers, employees can declare that they are representing/have an interest in the company, e.g. if writing product reviews.

A company's ability to meet fair competition guidelines can be jeopardised by employees using social media on behalf of the company; for example, if an employee, whilst representing the company, 'takes matters into their own hands' and uses social media unethically, to discredit the reputation of their employer's competitors.

Recruitment practices

A 2011 survey of 800 recruiters and human resource professionals found that 64% make use of two or more social networks as part of their assessment practices when recruiting employees. There are also specialist organisations that provide social media employment screening services. This raises ethical challenges for employers around an employee's right to privacy and fairness. Is it ethical or fair to judge an individual's ability to fulfil their employee responsibilities based on information about their personal lives, gained from their social media profile? In some cases, the information may relate to past activities in a job candidate's personal life. An Ethikos article cited a case where an individual was denied a job due to his activities posted online 20 years' previously.

Where an employer does use social media in recruitment screening/assessment of potential employees, whether this is done directly or outsourced, the company should have a clear policy and be open about it.

Duty of care

As highlighted previously, social media blurs the boundaries between personal and work life. When personal opinions expressed through social media (either on a personal profile or an online forum) refer to a company, it raises an ethical challenge. It is unclear what control, if any, the company has over comments communicated in this way and what action it can/should take.

The blurring of personal- and work-life boundaries can make it difficult for companies to uphold their duty of care to employees. For example, it is hard to monitor cases of 'cyber-bullying', particularly where employees use their personal social media account. One in ten UK workers believes that workplace cyber-bullying is a problem and a fifth of employers have had to discipline staff for posting nasty comments about a colleague online. The same survey found bullying and harassment and discrimination were two of the top five risks of social media for the workplace. The challenge for companies is identifying acceptable levels of monitoring employees' personal use of social media, without being seen to limit their freedom of expression – see Box 2 for examples.

Companies which choose to monitor employees' personal use of social media need to communicate their policy to employees so that they are aware of the practice, what it means for employees, and why it is necessary. Clear guidance is needed to help regulate monitoring and set its boundaries to avoid potential abuses.

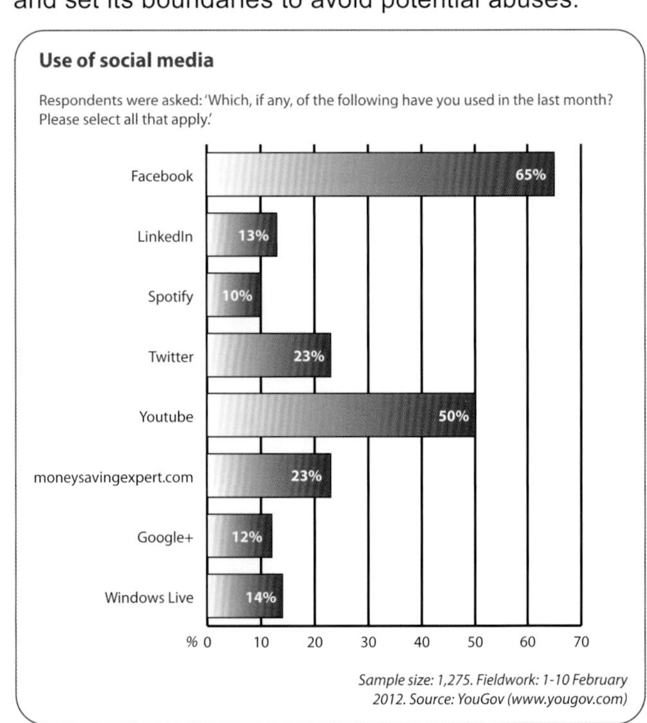

Sample size: 1,275. Fieldwork: 1-10 February 2012. Source: YouGov (www.yougov.com)

INSTITUTE OF BUSINESS ETHICS

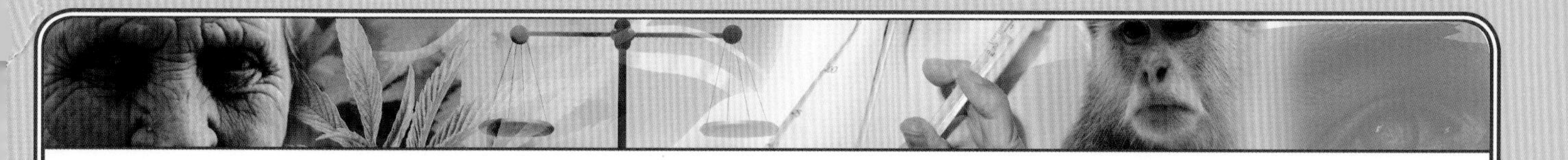

Box 2: Monitoring social media use – corporate examples

Serco Group

'The key question is can we and should we (ethically) be enforcing our corporate policies relating to our employees (linked in many cases to our core values as an organisation) outside of work?

'In a recent case a member of the public complained to us that the views on an employee's Facebook page (potentially racist) were not in line with our company values and because they had listed us as their employer, basically the question was "What are we going to do about it?" The information in that case was clearly not being discussed in a work context, the only link being that the individual worked for us – BUT, where do you draw the line? Should our policies prevent them from working for us?

'Therefore the company has reserved the right to monitor such activity, and this is now highlighted in our code of conduct.'

Argos

In August 2011 Argos, the catalogue retail company, fired an employee for gross misconduct after he complained about his job on his Facebook page. The employee did not mention his employer in the comments, but the company maintained the comments breach the Argos social networking policy and could 'damage the reputation of the company'.

Providing guidance

To address the ethical challenges that social media presents, companies need to fully assess the risks and be aware of the challenges presented by social media before using it.

Through a social media policy companies can provide guidance to employees on how to address the ethical challenges. The policy needs to be consistent with the company's ethics policy and overlap with other existing policies around communication. The policy would provide guidance on two main areas: employees' use of social media on behalf of the company, and employees' personal use of social media, including issues such as bullying and harassment, speaking up and employees' rights to privacy.

The guidance could also make clear that employees are not judged for personal activities or opinions as long as they are within the law, not offensive to others or the company, and do not refer to the company or work life. Companies may advise employees on security settings for personal social media accounts, encouraging them to apply high privacy settings. Alternatively, companies may prefer employees to disclose their employer, to facilitate company monitoring practices. As one company's policy states: 'your responsibility to [the Company] doesn't end when you are off the clock'. Guidance might emphasise the need for employees to reflect on their individual responsibility to the company when using social media.

Guidance on social media needs to be reviewed and communicated more regularly than other policies due to the rapid pace of change and development in social media and its use. Of those companies with a social media policy, the majority are failing to effectively communicate, monitor and roll out training on the policy. KPMG releases regular alerts and communications to ensure personnel are aware of the social media policy and firm practice. When personnel navigate to a social media site, an on-screen alert appears to remind them of their individual responsibility to comply with firm policies.

Developing guidance

An effective social media policy is developed through engagement and dialogue between the employer and its employees. Engagement may be particularly useful for companies deciding whether to monitor employees' use of social media. This helps ensure guidance is reasonably fair and understood by and acceptable to both parties. Similarly, it can be beneficial for the ethics function to work with other functions across the organisation to develop an effective social media policy (see Box 3); for example, working with Human Resources and Corporate Affairs helps ensure guidance reflects the sensitivity of the topic.

It is also important for companies to manage external stakeholders' expectations about their engagement with the company's social media profile. This can be done through 'terms of use': e.g. stating whether the page is monitored or not, whether negative/racist comments, etc. will be removed, that views expressed are by fans and not endorsed by the company, and so on.

Box 3: Partnerships between functions

Shell

'Our Communications team are now in the process of developing, in collaboration with Ethics & Compliance, Legal, HR and Internal Risk Management, policies and standards to cover (a) internal use, to give employees clear guidance about what they should and should not do in social media, (b) external Terms of Use to set expectations with the external community on how the company will engage, and (c) a toolset for marketing that provides guidance on engagement processes.'

December 2011

⇨ Information from the Institute of Business Ethics. This and other business ethics briefings are available to download free from the IBE website: www.ibe.org.uk/index.asp?upid=51&msid=8

INSTITUTE OF BUSINESS ETHICS

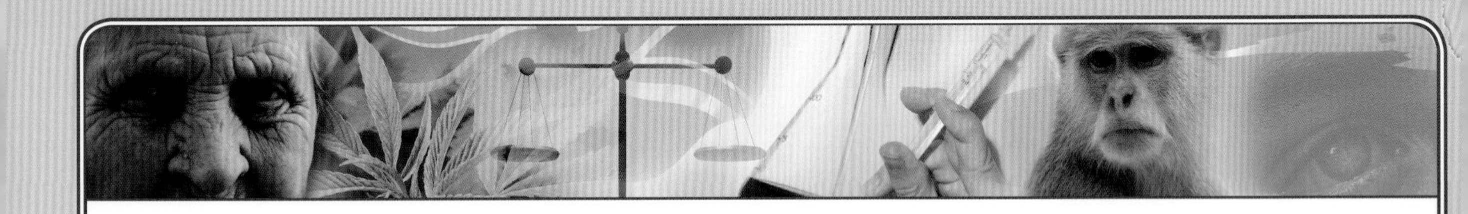

KEY FACTS

⇨ A recent report by Bibby Financial Services, *2020 Vision: The Future of Business*, predicts a 20% increase in the number of small businesses in the UK. (page 2)

⇨ London's global financial centre was ranked first in the 2011 Global Financial Centres Index. Across the UK, there are more than one million people employed in financial services. (page 3)

⇨ There were an estimated 4.5 million private sector businesses in the UK at the start of 2011, an increase of 94,000 (2.1 per cent) since the start of 2010. (page 4)

⇨ The number of businesses started in 2011 is up by 18 per cent on last year, research finds. (page 5)

⇨ There are 4.5 million small businesses in the UK. (page 6)

⇨ Latest Aviva SME Pulse reveals one in four small and medium enterprise (SME) owners are considering returning to the workforce as an employee. A third say they have lost the enthusiasm to run their own business. (page 8)

⇨ Nearly six in ten, 58%, of the British public believe business behaves very (4%) or fairly (54%) ethically. (page 11)

⇨ A survey of more than 2,000 members of the British public shows the overwhelming majority of people believe that businesses are 'good' for Britain as long as they comply with the law, pay their taxes, and make a profit (82%). (page 13)

⇨ 79% of survey respondents believe creating new jobs should be a high priority for UK firms, compared to generating a profit (43%). (page 14)

⇨ The average top salary in the FTSE 100 companies is about 300 times higher than the average salaries across those companies. (page 15)

⇨ £46 billion is the combined subsidy the 'Big Five' UK banks enjoyed in 2010. (page 16)

⇨ More than two-thirds (72%) of 2,000 people surveyed thought that a company's first priority should be to its workforce; less than a third said its shareholders should come first. (page 17)

⇨ Average annual charitable donations by a FTSE 100 company amount to something less than one-fifth of one per cent of profits. (page 21)

⇨ Average remuneration for the 1,200 most senior staff in financial services was £1.8 million in 2010, which means that pay for a single City worker in that group is equal to the total income of 69 families on capped benefits. (page 26)

⇨ The World Bank and the World Economic Forum suggest that corruption adds 10% to the total cost of doing business globally, and a staggering 25% to the cost of procurement contracts in developing countries. (page 31)

⇨ Tax avoidance is legal. Tax avoidance exploits the loopholes in tax law to ensure that less tax is paid than those creating that legislation expected. (page 32)

⇨ Christian Aid estimate that tax dodging by multinationals costs developing countries some $160 billion a year in lost tax revenue – 1.5 times the amount they receive from rich countries in aid. (page 33)

⇨ Europe as a whole loses the equivalent of 87% of its total healthcare budget to tax evasion, while Africa loses 98% and South America 139%. (page 34)

⇨ The banking sector makes heaviest use of tax havens, with a total of 1,649 tax haven companies between the 'big four' banks. (page 35)

⇨ A 2011 survey found social media is used for personal and work-related activities by 95% of employees. (page 37)

GLOSSARY

Capitalism

An economic system in which wealth generation is driven by privately-owned enterprises and individuals, rather than the state.

Corporate social responsibility

Corporate social responsibility, or CSR, is a concept closely linked to business ethics. It refers to self-regulation by a business or corporation, which is built into their overall business model. Companies which are serious about CSR will conduct their business in an ethical way and in the interests of the wider community (and society at large).

Entrepreneur

An individual who starts and runs their own business.

'Fat cats'

A term used to describe business owners and corporation heads perceived as having received rich rewards beyond their just deserts (e.g. large bonuses).

Free market

Any market in which price is decided by supply and demand. A free market economy would not be constrained by taxation, regulation or trade barriers.

FTSE 100

The 100 wealthiest companies listed on the London stock exchange.

Globalisation

Globalisation is a term used to explain the increased social and trade-related exchanges between nations. It implies that nations are moving closer together economically and culturally.

Gross Domestic Product (GDP)

The value of all the goods and services produced in a country within a year.

Recession

A period during which economic activity has slowed, causing a reduction in Gross Domestic Product (GDP), employment, household incomes and business profits. If GDP shows a reduction over at least six months, a country is then said to be in recession. Recessions are caused by people spending less, businesses making less and banks being more reluctant to give people loans.

Shareholder

Anyone who owns shares in a company or corporation.

SMEs

This stands for small and medium-sized enterprises. It describes any company with fewer than 250 employees.

Stakeholder

Anyone who has an interest in the behaviour and performance of a business. This does not necessarily mean a shareholder or investor: members of the community and society in general might also be said to have a stake in a business if the company's actions and behaviour will affect them.

Tax avoidance

Tax avoidance is any attempt by a corporation to reduce the amount of tax they are required to pay by the state. Unlike tax evasion, which seeks to illegally avoid paying tax, tax avoidance does not break the law: rather, it exploits legal loopholes to lessen tax.

Tax haven

Any territory offering a low rate of taxation. By locating their subsidiary companies in these territories, corporations are able to benefit from these low rates, thereby avoiding paying higher amounts of tax to the state in which their main base of operations is located. Well-known tax havens include Switzerland, New Zealand and the Cayman Islands.

Turnover

The total amount of business done in a given time.

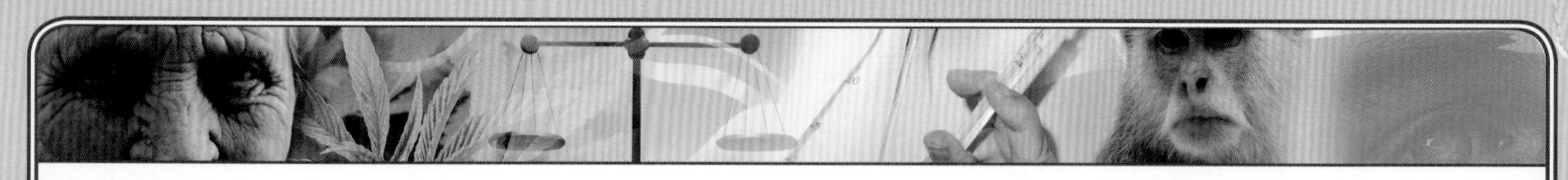

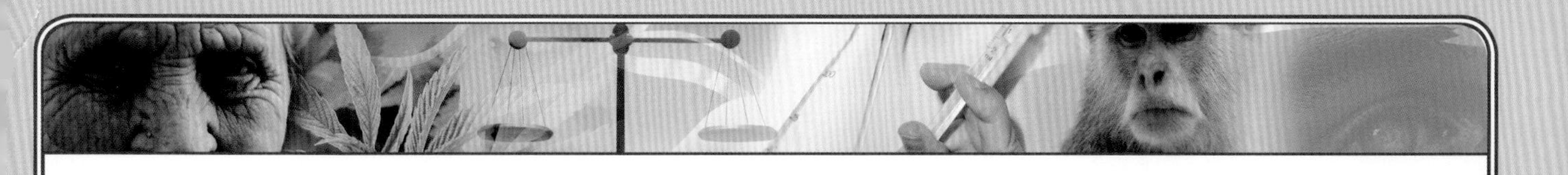

ACKNOWLEDGEMENTS

The publisher is grateful for permission to reproduce the following material.

While every care has been taken to trace and acknowledge copyright, the publisher tenders its apology for any accidental infringement or where copyright has proved untraceable. The publisher would be pleased to come to a suitable arrangement in any such case with the rightful owner.

Chapter One: Business in the UK

Brave new world of business, © Recruiter, *UK economy key facts,* © Crown copyright is reproduced with the permission of Her Majesty's Stationery Office, *Businesses in the UK,* © Crown copyright is reproduced with the permission of Her Majesty's Stationery Office, *Start-ups on the rise in UK,* © SmallBusiness.co.uk, *Young people aspire to be entrepreneurs,* © SmallBusiness.co.uk, *Small business statistics,* © Federation of Small Businesses, *PM challenges potential entrepreneurs to unleash the 'Business in You',* © startups, *UK entrepreneurial spirit under pressure,* © Aviva.

Chapter Two: Corporate Responsibility

Corporate social responsibility, © tutor2u, *Surveys on business ethics, 2011,* © Institute of Business Ethics, *A world in trust,* © Echo Research and International Business Leaders Forum 2010, *Business is a force for good, says British public,* © British Chambers of Commerce, *Anti-business?,* © Trades Union Congress, *Key facts,* © Occupy Bristol, *In an age of austerity, can capitalism really be popular?,* © Guardian News & Media Ltd 2012, *Mind your own business,* © The Spectator, *We must still reward success, says Cridland,* © CBI, *We need a New Philanthropy for the 21st century,* © Telegraph Media Group Limited 2011, *Why do good companies do bad things?,* © Guardian News & Media Ltd 2012, *Just deserts, or good luck?,* © Ipsos MORI, *Cap bonuses, not benefits,* © New Economics Foundation, *Business and human rights,* © Business and Human Rights Resource Centre, *Forced labour,* © Maplecroft in partnership with the United Nations Global Compact, *Why eliminating corruption is crucial to sustainability,* © Guardian News & Media Ltd 2012, *Tax and corporate responsibility,* © Tax Research UK, *Investors should make tax an ethical issue,* © Christian Aid, *Huge cost of tax evasion revealed as campaign to tackle tax havens launches,* © Tax Justice Network, *Addicted to tax havens,* © ActionAid, *The ethical challenges of social media,* © Institute of Business Ethics.

Illustrations

Pages 1, 13, 21, 29: Simon Kneebone; pages 7, 16, 23, 32: Don Hatcher; pages 8, 15: Bev Aisbett; pages 12, 18, 24, 37: Angelo Madrid.

Cover photography

Left: © Michał Koralewski. Centre: © Simon Rogers. Right: © Steve Woods/rgbstock.com.

Additional acknowledgements

With thanks to the Independence team: Cara Acred, Mary Chapman, Sandra Dennis and Jan Sunderland.

Lisa Firth
Cambridge
April, 2012

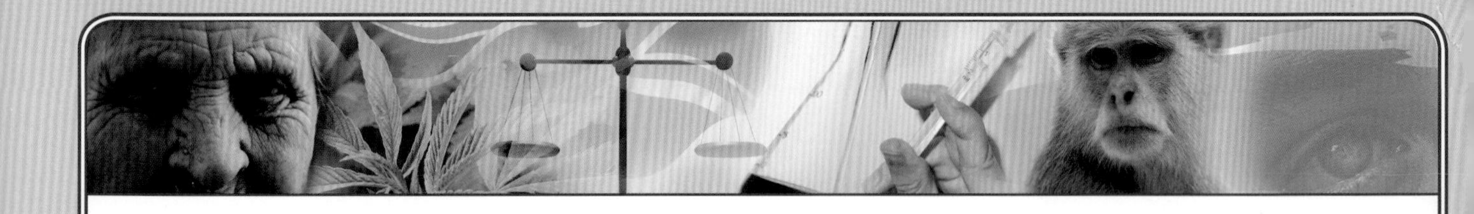

ASSIGNMENTS

The following tasks aim to help you think through the debates surrounding business ethics and provide a better understanding of the topic.

1 In groups, stage your own version of the television programme 'The Apprentice'.

2 'High flyers in the financial industry are required to take large risks as part of their job: it is only right they should receive large bonuses in recompense. If we do not reward success, talented wealth creators will move elsewhere.' Debate this statement in pairs, with each taking a different view.

3 Read *Brave new world of business* on pages 1-3. What do you think the future of business will be? Write a short story which describes business and working conditions in the year 2060.

4 Make a list of the benefits and risks associated with becoming an entrepreneur. Would you ever consider starting your own business?

5 Choose one of the following notable entrepreneurs: Richard Branson, Bill Gates, Steve Jobs, Anita Roddick, Mark Zuckerberg. Following your own research, write a short biography describing their life and work.

6 Read *Cap bonuses, not benefits* on page 26. Do you agree that benefits claimants have been unfairly scapegoated during the economic crisis?

7 'It is not fair that companies are able to avoid paying tax through the use of tax havens. If they enjoy the services offered by the country in which their main operations are based, it is only right they should contribute by paying full taxes.' Do you agree? Can you also see the viewpoint of businesses who use tax havens? Write an article which outlines your views on this issue.

8 'There is one and only one social responsibility of business – to use its resources and engage in activities designed to increase its profit so long as it stays within the rules of the game, which is to say, engages in open and free competition, without deception or fraud.' Milton Friedman, American economist. Discuss this quotation in small groups. Following your discussion, take a vote on whether you agree or disagree with Mr Friedman's analysis.

9 Choose a large company you are aware of – for example, a clothing retailer, supermarket or chain restaurant you have used in the past – and use their website and other sources to research their policy on corporate social responsibility. In addition, find out about their record on ethical issues such as human rights. Create a Powerpoint presentation about the company you have chosen and deliver it to your class.

10 Imagine you are the CEO of a large company. How would you integrate corporate social responsibility into your business model? Come up with ten rules which would ensure your business operates ethically, sustainably and responsibly.

11 Read *Surveys on business ethics, 2011*, on page 11. Create and conduct a similar survey within your year group. Do most people feel that British businesses behave ethically? Present your findings as a set of graphs.

12 Watch the 1987 film 'Wall Street' starring Michael Douglas. Write a review, focusing on the character of Bud and the choices he makes as he pursues his career.

13 What is 'greenwashing'? Write a short description of this practice and why it is damaging.

14 Use the online archives of at least two different UK newspapers to research the Occupy movement. Has the press coverage of this campaign been mainly positive or negative? Do different newspapers take different views? What sense does the press coverage give of the Occupy protests' effectiveness?

15 Use the Internet to research a notable 19th-century philanthropist such as George Cadbury, Titus Salt or Joseph Rowntree. Write a summary, outlining how these business owners worked their philanthropic agenda into their overall business model.